NO CROSS, NO CROWN

NO CROSS, NO CROWN

Philip Edgcumbe Hughes

Embrace Christ's cross, and Christ shall embrace you.
—Hugh Latimer, bishop and martyr

MOREHOUSE-BARLOW
Wilton, Connecticut

l

Morehouse-Barlow Co., Inc.
78 Danbury Road
Wilton, Connecticut 06897

Library of Congress Cataloging-in-Publication Data

Hughes, Philip Edgcumbe.
   No cross, no crown / Philip Edgcumbe Hughes.
      p.   cm.
   1. Temptation—Meditations.   I. Title.
BT725.H86 1988   8T-29353
248.4—dc 19   CIP

ISBN 0-8192-1423-X

Printed in the United States of America
by
BSC Litho
Harrisburg, PA

Contents

Introduction

The road taken by Christ for our redemption was the road that led necessarily from Bethlehem to Calvary and from Calvary to his enthronement as Lord of all in the glory that he had left to come to our assistance. To bypass the cross would have defeated the purpose of his coming. His whole way on earth was the way of the cross, that is to say, the way of conflict with temptation, of suffering, and of death. Moreover, his contest with the power of evil was waged in his life as well as in his death. In the pages that follow we shall consider the nature and meaning of the temptations that Jesus faced and overcame and then the significance of his victory for us as we daily have our faith tested by temptation in its various forms. Finally, the victorious power that flows from him to us will be illustrated by recalling the lives and deaths of some who, impelled by devotion to their Redeemer, have in different ages given inspiring proof of the genuineness of their faith at the cost of affliction and suffering. The gospel to which they were faithful witnesses is the same gospel for which, as Paul said of himself, "I am suffering and wearing fetters like a criminal." They knew full well what he meant. And they also believed, as he believed, that "if we have died with Christ we shall also live with him, if we endure we shall also reign with him, if we deny him he also will deny us" (2 Tim. 2:9, 11f.). They persevered to the end, as Paul did, fighting the good fight, finishing the race, keeping the faith, and, attributing all the glory to God and his grace, they looked forward to receiving the crown of life that awaited them (2 Tim. 4:7f.). In short, they learned, as all true followers of Christ must learn, that if there is no cross there is no crown.

On Being Tempted

Temptation is the inducement or the inclination to do what we know to be wrong. It is experienced daily by Christians. To be tempted is not in itself wrong or sinful. This is evident from the fact that our incarnate Redeemer who did no wrong endured temptation. As we read in Heb. 4:15, he was "in every respect . . . tempted as we are, yet without sinning." In other words, he consistently overcame temptation. The outcome of temptation is either victory or defeat, and it is our being overcome by temptation instead of overcoming it that results in wrongdoing.

It would, of course, be absurd to imagine that God, who in Christ has redeemed us from sin and provided us with the power to overcome temptation, is the one who tempts us to commit sin. "Let no one say when he is tempted, 'I am tempted by God,' " James wrote, "for God cannot be tempted with evil and he himself tempts no one; but each person is tempted when he is lured and enticed by his own desire" (James 1:13f.). The desire to do wrong that temptation arouses may come from our environment ("the world") or from the lusting of our heart within ("the flesh") or from Satan who is the great opponent of godliness ("the devil")—or most likely from a combination of all three. Hence the historic baptismal renunciation of "the devil and all his works, the vain pomp and glory of the world, with all covetous desires of the same, and the sinful desires of the flesh," and the prayer that the one baptized "may have power and strength to have victory, and to triumph, against the devil, the world, and the flesh."

To be tempted is to be tested. Each temptation comes to us as a challenge to stand firm and be faithful, as a step to be climbed rather than an occasion for falling, as an opportunity for blessing rather than for surrender to the shame and guilt of defeat. Thus James assures us, "Blessed is the man who endures temptation [that is, without giving in to it], for when he has stood the test he will receive the crown of life which God has promised to those who love him" (James 1:12). The secret of victory, however, is not in ourselves but in the strength supplied by Christ, the great overcomer of all temptation (Heb. 2:18; 4:15f.).

The Temptations of Jesus

The tempting of Jesus, and in particular his complete victory over temptation, was an essential preliminary to the cross. To understand this we must grasp the significance of Jesus as the last or second Adam whose coming was designed to undo the evil that resulted from the temptation and defeat of the first Adam (1 Cor. 15:45ff.). This meant, first of all, that the defeat of the first Adam had to be counteracted by the victory over temptation of the second Adam. It was essential for our salvation that human nature that was tested and failed in the first Adam should be tested and gain the victory in Christ. Only thus could Christ go to the cross as one who had established the perfection of his own righteousness (cf. Heb. 2:10); only thus could he be qualified to die there for us sinners, "the righteous for the unrighteous" (1 Pet. 3:18). Had the incarnate Son given way to but a single temptation or failed even in the least degree, he would have incapacitated himself to fulfill the function of our Savior; he would (unthinkable as it is to us) himself have been in need of salvation. The victory of our Lord's death on the cross, the severest testing of all, would have been of no avail had it not been preceded by the victory of his life in the facing and surmounting of every other temptation.

As the first man was created a human being of innocence and wholeness, with the potential for advancing in harmony with the Creator's will to the consummating glory that is humanity's true destiny, so also at his incarnation the Son was born into this world in a state of spotless integrity, in accordance with the annunciation made to his virgin mother: "The Holy Spirit will come upon you, and the power of the Most High will overshadow you; therefore the child to be born will be called holy, the Son of God" (Luke 1:35). Thus he became our fellow human being, uniting our nature to himself, and started his human existence in the same holy purity as that in which the first Adam was formed. Though the main purpose of the birth at Bethlehem was the death at Calvary, for "the Son of Man . . . came . . . to give his life as a ransom for many" (Mark 10:45), it was necessary that the years between the cradle and the cross should, in contrast to the first Adam, be distinguished by total conquest of temptation so that he might not only die our death but do so, as we have said, by offering himself up as the innocent substitute for the guilty. As Paul puts it, "in Christ God was reconciling the world to himself" and "for our sake he made him to be sin who knew no sin, so that in him we might become the righteousness of God" (2 Cor. 5:19, 21). The whole purpose of the incarnation was our redemption and rehabilitation, and our attainment, in Christ, of that incomparable glory that is our true destiny.

Some have maintained that there was no possibility of Christ's being defeated by temptation. But if this were so it would rob his temptations of all genuine force and significance. They would not have been occasions that truly tested his resolution; indeed, they would have been no more real than exhibitions of shadowboxing without an authentic opponent. True, it is inconceivable to us who know him as our victorious champion that he should have failed and fallen, for then our whole redemption would have been lost, and the devil would be supreme as Christ's conqueror. This consideration, however, underscores the importance of our Lord's conflict being a real conflict with the powers of evil. An unreal conflict would have meant a bogus and a powerless victory of no worth to us in our need for a true champion. As the conflict of the first Adam was real and his defeat real, so the conflict of the second Adam had to be real and his victory real; otherwise there is no proper correspondence and contrast.

In our own experience we know very well that the conflict with temptation is an intensely real conflict. We have also the apostolic teaching of the New Testament that Christ was "in every respect . . . tempted as we are, yet without sinning" (Heb. 4:15), and this is a sufficient assurance to us of the reality of his temptations. Moreover, the agony of Gethsemane and the cross, which was the awful climax of his testing, affords incontestable proof of the terrible reality of the force against which he had to do battle. The genuine temptability of Christ

2

is a true indication of the genuineness of his fellow humanity with us. The temptations he endured and overcame were a real assault on the integrity of his humanity and posed a real threat to his holiness. Only because it was real and hard won is his victory a source of real strength and encouragement to us in our hour of testing (Heb. 2:18 and 4:15f. again!).

The wilderness temptations of our Lord as described in Matt. 4:1ff. come at the beginning of his earthly ministry, which led up to his crucifixion. The event immediately preceding them was his baptism in the river Jordan, when the voice from heaven proclaimed, "This is my beloved Son, with whom I am well pleased" (Matt. 3:16f.). As we shall see, this was an utterance that the devil attempted, in two of the three temptations, to manipulate to his own advantage.

We are told, further, that after his baptism "Jesus was led up by the Spirit into the wilderness to be tempted by the devil" (Matt. 4:1). This clearly implies that the conquest of temptation and the defeat of the tempter by the second Adam was an important element in the fulfillment of his mission to our world. His ministry commenced as it would also conclude in head-to-head combat with the great enemy who is bent on our destruction.

And the enemy's attack came when Jesus had been without food for forty days and forty nights and his life-force was at a low ebb (Matt. 4:2). The assault was timed to coincide with what promised to be his moment of greatest vulnerability. Jesus was alone, physically enfeebled, far removed from all human support, when the devil came to destroy him and with him our salvation. But, at the same time, Jesus was there to do battle with the devil for our sakes. The scene was as dramatic as the warfare was earnest. The issue at stake was our eternal destiny.

The First Wilderness Temptation

The first of these temptations in the wilderness took the form of an invitation to perform a straightforward miracle: "If you are the Son of God, command these stones to become loaves of bread" (Matt. 4:3). The first thing to be noticed here is the connection with the declaration of the voice from heaven at Jesus' baptism, "This is my beloved Son, with whom I am well pleased." After fasting for forty days Jesus was hungry and exhausted, in a condition of extreme physical weakness, and even to all appearances close to death. In no way did he look like the Son of God; indeed, quite the contrary. The thrust of Satan's temptation was this, that the demonstration of the possession of the miraculous power to transform stones into bread would afford proof, contrary to all appearances, that Jesus was indeed the Son of God, as the voice had asserted. Furthermore, the inducement to provide bread in this way had every semblance of being sensible and realistic: it would be a wise emergency measure calculated to strengthen Jesus by providing bread for him to eat. Thus strengthened he would, commendably, prevent himself from dying alone and unnoticed in the desert, his mission unfulfilled. Considered in this light, the implication was that there was every justification for adopting this course of action as an emergency measure. But if such a step were not taken and Jesus were to succumb to starvation, not only would the purpose of his coming be overthrown but also the voice from heaven would be falsified, and that would be doubly disastrous.

It was, in effect, an appeal to "common sense," suggesting the necessity both for self-preservation and for the demonstration of the accuracy of the word spoken from above. Perceived in this way, it looked as though by performing this simple miracle Jesus had everything to gain and nothing to lose. And therein lay the subtlety of this apparently harmless, indeed apparently benevolent, invitation; for had our Lord acceded to the devil's prompting, it was he who would have lost all and the devil who would have won the ascendancy. For what Satan was really doing was to sow in Christ's mind the seed of doubt not only regarding his own identity but also regarding the trustworthiness of the word spoken by God. All the circumstantial appearances seemed to support Satan's qualification, "*If* you are the Son of God"; but it was a qualification that immediately cast doubt on the veracity of the divine word and, in effect, denied it.

The word from heaven, because it is *God's* word, is absolutely true and reliable. God's word is always truth (John 17:17). It is given for our assurance and sanctification. But the devil's method has always been to induce doubt and disbelief and to destroy confidence in God's word. It was so at the beginning, when the tempter turned a plain statement into a question, "Did God say . . .?" and then followed it with a flat denial, "You will not die . . ." (Gen. 2:17; 3:1-4). As truth

4

and life belong together, so also do their opposites, falsehood and death. Hence Christ's categorical denunciation of the devil: "He was a murderer from the beginning, and has nothing to do with the truth, because there is no truth in him. When he lies, he speaks according to his own nature, for he is a liar and the father of lies" (John 8:44).

God's word is not questionable. It leaves no room for "ifs" and queries. It is not altered by physical appearances and daunting circumstances, nor is its truth conditional on our approval or cooperation. We should notice that in this and the following temptations Christ did not parley with Satan or debate the issue with him. He gave no encouragement to the notion that the clear utterance of God might be susceptible of a variety of interpretations or might need to be bent to suit a particular situation. On the contrary, Christ made plain his absolute confidence in the trustworthiness of God's word by his direct quotation of Scripture: "It is written. . . ."—and he did this on all three occasions, thereby indicating that the truth of God is inflexible and that this is the means available to us for repulsing the tempter when he seeks to destroy our faith with suggestions of doubt and disbelief.

It was with the sword of the Spirit (Eph. 6:17) that Jesus made his counterthrust, quoting the admonition of Deut. 8:3, "It is written, 'Man shall not live by bread alone, but by every word that proceeds from the mouth of God.' " The absolute necessity for life is God's word of truth, and that word is in no way dependent on the supply of bread in the wilderness for its validation. Bread is of merely subsidiary importance; the acceptance of the devil's proposal would have made it of primary importance. And that would have been a suicidal policy. For it is, not bread, but the word of God that brought all things into existence and keeps them in existence, and it is God's word, not bread, that gives meaning and purpose to our existence. Anxiety about survival is not compatible with reliance on the word of God. To this, without regard to his physical weakness, our Lord bore witness in the wilderness, and also later on in his teaching, when he said, "Do not be anxious about your life, what you shall eat, nor about your body, what you shall put on. For life is more than food, and the body more than clothing." The principle he affirmed and personified was that of complete childlike confidence in our heavenly Father who lovingly and constantly cares for us

5

and whose good pleasure it is to give us the kingdom (Luke 12:22ff.).

The devil's temptation was a sort of commercial, designed to convince Jesus of the advantages to be gained by putting material things first. It is a temptation with which Satan has had, and continues to have, outstanding success. We well know this in our day when the different media of communication bombard us incessantly with commercials inciting us to improve our lives by the acquisition of material luxuries and indulgence in temporal pleasures, and assuring us that lottery tickets hold the promise of instant happiness. Many are persuaded to their ultimate disillusionment, that it is "by bread alone" that we shall live, that life and materialistic gratification are synonymous.

There is a lesson for us to learn also from Christ's use of Scripture: the passage he cited from Deut. 8:3 was appropriate not simply in itself but also by reason of its setting in a wilderness context. The words here and in the quotations with which Jesus rebutted the next two temptations are the words spoken by Moses to the Israelites in the wilderness as their forty years of wandering came to an end. "You shall remember all the way which the LORD your God has led you these forty years in the wilderness, that he might humble you, testing you to know what was in your heart," Moses said. And he reminded them that, contrary to all human possibilities, God had unfailingly provided for their material needs and physical sustenance (Deut. 8:2–4). Jesus was, in effect, telling the devil that the same God would not fail to provide for his incarnate Son after forty days in the wilderness. Against such firmness of faith and confidence it would have been futile for Satan to have pressed this temptation further.

There is, however, no justification for concluding that this temptation was unappealing to Jesus. After forty days without food he was in a state of starvation, and the prospect of having bread to eat must then have been strongly attractive to him. The important thing for Jesus was to penetrate beyond the surface appearance of his situation to the deep motive that lay at the heart of this temptation. That motive was to bring about the overturning of the mission of our salvation that Christ had come to accomplish. The hidden intention was to persuade our Lord to put self first, for that is what putting bread first would have meant. The implied logic was that by putting himself first at this juncture Jesus would understandably be preserving himself to fulfill the redeeming work he had come to do. This seemingly worthy objective also lent strength to the temptation.

But for Jesus to have put self first even for a moment would have defeated the whole purpose of his coming to us. His true food was the performance of the will of the Father, not his own will. The bread of this world could never be given priority or be a substitute for this. This he made plain to his disciples on another occasion when he was fatigued and hungry; for when they brought him food and besought him to eat he said, "I have food to eat of which you do not know. . . . My food is to do the will of him who sent me, and to accomplish his work" (John 4:6, 31–34). Moreover, for him to have acceded to the temptation to save himself in the wilderness would have been subversive of his mission because it was us, not himself, whom he came to save. "The Son of man came," he declared, "not to be served [or to be self-serving] but to serve, and to give his life as a ransom for many" (Matt. 20:28). Saving his life would have been the very opposite of giving his life!

But, in addition to all this, Jesus himself is the true Word of God (John 1:1), God's last Word and saving Word (Heb. 1:1–3), the personal Word to whom the written word testifies (John 5:39), the unique Word proceeding from God by which we are to live. His coming for our salvation was precisely the emptying of self (Phil. 2:7), the way of total self-abnegation. By descending to the lowest depths of our fallenness he has recovered for us the true image and destiny of our creation. To have served self by turning stones into bread in the wilderness would have been the ruination of his mission and our salvation.

The Son, as we have said, did not come to provide bread for himself but bread for us—the true bread for us to eat and thus live forever. This truth is memorably expounded in the great discourse in John 6, where Jesus reveals that he is the God-given Bread by which we are to live. This is all the more dramatic because it is a teaching that stands in unmistakable contrast to the bread of this world that he had miraculously provided for the hungry five thousand, who were now pressing upon him in the hope that he would gratify their desire for more wonders of this kind (John 6:1ff., 22ff.). But to them he now declared a far more wonderful truth: "I am the bread of life; he who comes to me shall not hunger, and he who believes in me shall never thirst" (John 6:35); and also: "I am the living bread which came down from heaven; if any one eats of this bread, he will live for ever; and the bread which I shall give for the life of the world is my flesh" (John 6:51). In other words, it is by coming to Christ Jesus in faith that we feed on the bread of life, and the making available of this living bread to us was by the incarnate Son's giving of his flesh in our place in his death on the cross.

Therefore we should be eternally grateful to our Lord for his steadfast resistance to the devil's enticements. Had the tempter had the success with the last Adam that he had with the first, all would have been lost. It may indeed be said that the devil's very life depended on the repetition now of that first victory in this confrontation with the second Adam. And he will be persistent. But his is the desperation of a doomed creature, for the Son of God appeared for this very purpose, "to destroy the works of the devil" (1 John 3:8).

The Second Wilderness Temptation

Though the location of Jesus in the wilderness remains unchanged, there is a change of scene for the second temptation. We read that "the devil took him to the holy city, and set him on the pinnacle of the temple" (Matt. 4:5). We can readily picture the spectacle on which Jesus gazed from the high vantage point: the restless crowds of men, women, and children in the great courtyards below, many with deep yearnings for the coming of their long-promised Messiah, many others confused and burdened with the cares and problems of this life, and all in need of the salvation that he was there to bring them. This formed the setting for Satan's next invitation: "If you are the Son of God, throw yourself down." This invitation was accompanied by a scriptural quotation: "For it is written, 'He will give his angels charge of you,' and 'On their hands they will bear you up, lest you strike your foot against a stone' " (Matt. 4:6; Ps. 91:11f.).

Once again the devil casts doubt on the truthfulness of the utterance from heaven, "This is my beloved Son, with whom I am well pleased" (Matt. 3:17). Implicit in this temptation is the suggestion that if Jesus was unwilling to confirm to himself by turning stones into bread that he was the Son of God he should at least prove it to the people below by leaping without harm into their midst. It would be a convincing demonstration

8

to them that he was the promised Son and Messiah. And Satan bolstered the invitation with a passage from Scripture that promised divine protection. In doing this, he cleverly attempted to use the very weapon that Christ had used against him, with the implication that he was simply asking him to do something that was thoroughly in accord with the word of God and its assurances. Was not Christ caught in his own trap? How could he now repudiate or circumvent the authority to which he himself had appealed?

This should at least be a warning to us that the devil, too, can quote Scripture and in a manner that seems convincing. And if we are wise we will judge it altogether improbable that the devil would use Scripture except to his own advantage as one who implacably hates the truth of God. From this incident we should learn that there is a right way and a wrong way of quoting Scripture: either as our Lord did, "rightly handling the word of truth" (2 Tim. 2:15), or, as the devil did, wresting and misapplying the same word of truth (2 Pet. 3:16). Satan tore the text from its context, without regard for the unity of Scripture and its absolute reliability as the word of God; and this is the method of all false teachers, who are Satan's mouthpieces. It is also the method of some orthodox believers, who pick a verse here and a verse there because it pleases them or treat the Bible as a sort of lucky dip and show little respect for the profitability and coherence of Scripture in all its parts. If this is our method, we will never be able effectively to refute false teachings for which biblical authority is claimed. Hence the importance of studying the Bible in its entirety.

When we turn to Psalm 91, from which the devil extracted his quotation, we find that it is an affirmation of complete trust in God in every perilous circumstance of life. The majestic measures open with the assertion that "he who dwells in the shelter of the Most High, who abides in the shadow of the Almighty, will say to the Lord, 'My refuge and my fortress.' " And the psalmist hymns God as the great deliverer of those who make him their refuge in the time of deadly pestilence and in every menacing situation. The psalm offers no encouragement to rush irresponsibly into peril or to seek an overt demonstration of its promises. Yet the devil incited Jesus to place himself in peril by the commission of a rash deed for the purpose of proving both that he was the Son of God and also that the promise of angelic protection was true. But to presume to put to the test in this way the word of God, whether spoken through the psalmist or at the baptism, would be to abandon the scriptural principle of faith for the satanic principle of sight. God's word does not have to be tried out before it can be believed. Precisely because it is *God's* word it is true and cannot fail; it is sufficient in itself. God's word is always God's work (Isa. 55:11).

A striking illustration of faith in the word alone was given by the Roman centurion who came to Jesus with the entreaty that he would heal his servant who was gravely ill and who, when Jesus said, "I will come and heal him," replied, "Lord, I am not worthy to have you come under my roof, but only say the word, and my servant will be healed." Not only was the centurion commended for the exceptional strength of his faith, but the sufficiency of his faith in the Lord's word alone was attested by the fact that his servant was healed at the very moment when Jesus said, "Go; be it done for you as you have believed" (Matt. 8:5–13).

Jesus, let us note, did not wrangle with Satan over Scripture, which, being God's word of truth, had no place on the lips of him who is the father of lies. He conclusively settled the issue by repeating the decisive formula "It is written" to introduce the admonition, again from the wilderness oration of Moses, "You shall not put the LORD your God to the test" (Deut. 6:16). For Jesus to throw himself down from the pinnacle of the temple, as the devil proposed, would have been to put God to the test, with special reference in this instance to the promise of Ps. 91:11f. The manner of our Lord's response teaches us to respect the unity and integrity of Scripture in such a way that one passage may interpret another and that no place may be so expounded as to be repugnant to another.*

But there was more to the temptation than this; otherwise why did Satan invite Jesus to throw himself down from the pinnacle of the temple rather than from a crag in the desert, which would have served just as well to test the reliability of Psalm 91? To answer this, we need to picture the scene once again on which Jesus looked from that height: the milling multitude intent on worship and sacrifice, whose hope for his

---

*See the Twentieth of the Thirty-nine Articles of Religion (printed at the back of *The Book of Common Prayer*).

coming he was there at last to fulfill; people restless and insecure, like sheep in need of a shepherd. It was a sight that never failed to move him to compassion. Thus we read that, on a later occasion, "when he saw the crowds, he had compassion for them, because they were harassed and helpless, like sheep without a shepherd" (Matt. 9:36), and again at another time, when "he saw a great throng . . . he had compassion on them" (Matt. 14:14), and yet again, at the time of his feeding the hungry four thousand, he said, "I have compassion on the crowd" (Matt. 15:32). So also now, as he is being tempted, the spectacle below must have stirred the very depth of his being with pity and loving desire.

No doubt the devil was well aware of this. The temptation was designed to penetrate to the incarnate Son's heart as it aroused the longing within him to descend and minister to the needs of this multitude. For it was them he had come to save; he was the One for whom they were looking and waiting; he was the answer to their hopes, the Good Shepherd who was there to call his sheep to himself. The effect of his miraculous descent can easily be imagined. His own would have received him and all would have followed him joyfully. The Jews were seeking a sign, and this would be an infallibly persuasive sign. Let us not think that this temptation was not powerfully attractive to our Savior. There was nothing attractive about the cross and all the shame and suffering associated with it.

This temptation was but another satanic attempt to subvert the purpose of Christ's coming, to isolate Bethlehem from Calvary, indeed to eliminate the cross altogether. The devil was appealing to him to minister, not now to self, but to others, in accordance with the purpose of his coming, but to do so self-pleasingly, through a shift that would save him from the pain of giving his life as a ransom for others (Mark 10:45). He was proposing a shortcut or bypass, a quick and easy road to the fulfillment of his mission that would instantly win the multitude's enthusiastic allegiance to him as their long-awaited Messiah. Thus his objective would be accomplished—and painlessly!

But despite all the horror and agony that going on to Calvary foreboded, Christ refused to be turned aside from the cross. He had come to be a redeemer, not a demagogue, and apart from giving himself to death as a ransom for us there could be no redemption. To have been no more than a popular leader would have frustrated all that the incarnation was intended to achieve. The sign he had come to give was not that of a spectacular leap from a height but the sign of his death, burial, and resurrection for the world's salvation (Matt. 12:38–40). And so he set his face "like a flint" to go to Jerusalem, not to win popularity, but to be rejected and put to death (cf. Isa. 50:7). And so, too, he would repeatedly instruct his disciples "that he must go to Jerusalem and suffer many things . . . and be killed, and on the third day be raised" (Matt. 16:21; 17:22f.; 20:17–19).

As with the first temptation, so now with the second, we should not overlook the appropriate significance of the context of the quotation adduced by our Lord from the Book of Deuteronomy. Moses, as before, was addressing the Israelites after forty years in the wilderness. In warning them, "You shall not put the LORD your God to the test," he added a reference, by way of illustration, to a particular event: "as you tested him at Massah" (Deut. 6:16). The occasion is described in Exod. 17:1–7. In the course of their wanderings, the Israelites came to Rephidim, where they pitched camp. Their rebellious and unbelieving spirit was all too plainly displayed by the bitterness of their complaints because they found no water there. In an attitude of homicidal fury they charged Moses with having brought them out of Egypt in order to let them and their children perish in the desert. Moses, for his part, asked them, "Why do you put the LORD to the test?" There was no excuse for such faithless and vindictive ingratitude, for God, true to his promise, had never failed to provide for their needs. Their hostile temper of unbelief and apostasy made no sense. Their mutinous hearts even caused them to express the terrible question "Is the LORD among us or not?"

Commanded by the Lord to take his rod and strike the rock at Horeb, Moses did so, and water gushed forth and the people drank. So yet once more the Lord mercifully sustained his people in the wilderness, despite their failure of trust and loyalty. But thereafter that place was known as Massah, which means "testing," and Meribah, which means "contention,"— "because of the faultfinding of the children of Israel, and because they put the LORD to the test by saying, 'Is the LORD among us or not?' " In this particular temptation of his in the wilderness, Jesus was, in effect, being incited by the devil to ask the same skeptical question as he watched the unshepherded crowds below: "Is the Lord among us or not?" and thus to create another Massah by putting God and his word to the test (specifically, the word at his baptism that he was God's beloved Son and the promise of Ps. 91). But Christ's presence here on earth was in itself the affirmative answer to this question. It was, as Matthew asserts, the fulfillment of the ancient prophecy "Behold, a virgin shall conceive and bear a son, and his name shall be called Emmanuel," which means precisely "God with us" (Matt. 1:23; Isa. 7:14). To the same effect John testifies that the Word who himself is God "became flesh and dwelt among us" (John 1:1, 14). In the person of the incarnate Son, and through his redemptive work, God's covenant promise to dwell in the midst of his people has become a present reality that will have its glorious consummation in the perfect harmony of the new heaven and earth hereafter. Then the assurance given by the great voice that John heard in his vision on the isle of Patmos will be everlastingly actualized: "Behold, the dwelling of God is with men. He will dwell with them, and they shall be his people, and God himself will be with them" (Rev. 21:3; cf. Lev. 26:11f.; Ezek. 37:26f.; Zech. 2:10f.). Meanwhile the risen Lord has declared, "I am with you always, to the close of the age" (Matt. 28:20) and "I will never fail you nor forsake you" (Heb. 13:5).

In his appearance as our fellow human being, Christ did not look like the Lord Emmanuel (cf. Isa. 53:2) any more than the rock in the wilderness looked as though it could be the source of water for the thirsting people. Christ indeed is "the spiritual Rock" of his people. It is from him that the water of divine grace flows freely to us. Paul even states categorically that the rock in the wilderness was Christ (1 Cor. 10:4)—in other words, what took place at Rephidim was indicative of the presence and power of Christ in the midst of the people.* Frequently in Scripture the Lord God is described as the Rock of his people, as, for example, in 2 Sam. 22:2, where David sings, "The LORD is my rock, and my fortress, and my deliverer, my God, my Rock, in whom I take refuge." As that wilderness rock was by God's order smitten with Moses' rod, so the incarnate Son, our Rock, came to be smitten with the

---

*Bishop Robertson and Alfred Plummer wrote of this passage as providing "unquestionable evidence of the Apostle's belief in the pre-existence of Christ"; see Commentary on the First Epistle of St. Paul to the Corinthians ICC, (Edinburgh: T. and T. Clark 1911), p. 201.

rod that should have smitten us, and that smiting took place on the cross of Calvary. From the smitten One on that cross there flows to us the full stream of God's grace for the quenching of our soul-thirst in the wilderness of our wandering lostness. Of that river of the water of life the thirsty are invited to drink freely (Rev. 22:1, 17), confident in the Lord's promise: "Whoever drinks of the water that I shall give him will never thirst, the water that I shall give him will become in him a spring of water welling up to eternal life" (John 4:14).

This concept of Christ as our Rock provided the inspiration for Augustus Toplady's famous hymn "Rock of Ages, Cleft for Me" and also, not to mention others, for the longing expressed by J. S. B. Monsell:

I hunger and I thirst;
Jesu, my manna be;
Ye living waters, burst
Out of the Rock for me!

But, once again, the road Jesus had to tread was the road that led to Calvary, for that was to be the place of his smiting. There was no salvation by the route of popular demagoguery, no life for us apart from his dying there in our stead, no bypassing of the cross if he was to accomplish the mission that brought him to our world.

The Third Wilderness Temptation

Matthew now records that the devil next took Jesus "to a very high mountain, and showed him all the kingdoms of the world and the glory of them," and that he said to him, "All these I will give you, if you will fall down and worship me" (Matt. 4:7-9). Satan projected, so to speak, a panoramic spectacle of the wealth and magnificence of this world's power structures for Jesus to admire; a dazzling spectacle of universal dominion and of the splendor of creation was stretched out before him. And Satan offered all this to Jesus for one little gesture of obeisance. To all intents and purposes it was the ultimate prize, the crowning reward. These wilderness temptations seem, indeed, to have been progressive in their scope. The appeal advanced from the personal to the national and from the national to the universal level. Christ was invited first to save himself, then to lead his people, and finally to gain the world. In the first two, the performance of miracles had been proposed: the turning of stones into bread and descending unharmed from a height. But in the third there is no suggestion of a miraculous demonstration, nor did the devil repeat the folly of attempting to trade scriptural quotations with Christ or insinuate that his enticement had the authoritative backing of the word of God.

But what sort of temptation was this? It could hardly have been an inducement to indulge in personal ambition and vainglory. For the splendor of this world was as nothing in comparison with the infinite and eternal glory that the incarnate Son had set aside in coming into this world. That glory was his before the world was made (John 17:5, 24) and was to be briefly manifested on another mountain top to Peter, James, and John at the time of his transfiguration (Mark 9:2ff.) so that they could testify, "we were eyewitnesses of his majesty . . . for we were with him on the holy mountain" and "we have beheld his glory, glory as of the only Son from the Father" (2 Pet. 1:16–18; John 1:14). The gaze of Jesus undoubtedly penetrated through the magnificence of all this world's kingdoms to the ugliness of the self-seeking and discontent by which human society is in its fallenness disfigured. The prospect of the possession of the world in this state would not have been a temptation for him.

Satan's intention, rather, was to induce Jesus to believe that here was his opportunity to achieve in an instant his own *ultimate* goal, namely, the restoration of the world and the establishment of his personal rule over it. His coming was for the purpose of saving the world and setting up his kingdom of peace and justice. The hidden inducement in this temptation was, once again, for him to turn away from the cross, to take another simpler and more congenial route for the gaining of this objective—a route, however, that, once again, would have overthrown the whole purpose of his coming. For the devil offered Jesus the *possession*, not the saving, of the world, and the world could only be possessed by being saved; its first need was to be *saved*. Satan was proposing the throne without the cross. But the enthronement could only take place by way of the crucifixion: first the cross and then the crown.

Yet, as with the preceding temptations, we must not imagine that this temptation was without force or appeal to Jesus. As we have said, the horror of the cross certainly held no attraction for him. Moreover, it was through him and for him that the world was made, and it was love for the world that brought

15

him down to us (Col. 1:16; John 1:3, 3:16). Indeed, he had come to take the world from Satan; so Satan was saying, in effect, "Take it! It's yours, provided you fulfill one trifling condition!" The suggestion was that his grand objective could be obtained at once, without delay and without pain.

If the question is asked what possible justification the devil had for making such a proposition to our Lord, the answer may be given that he had in a certain sense gained control of the world—not, however, by right but by usurpation and the ungodly will of all who wished to rid themselves of the rule of God over them. Satan was in fact a false god, a substitute deity set up in the place of the only true God, no more than a so-called god (cf. 1 Cor. 8:5f). The world in its fallenness has made the devil, who is a no-god, its god. That is why Jesus could speak of the devil as "the ruler of this world" (John 14:30) and why Paul could actually call him "the god of this world" (2 Cor. 4:4). To the same effect John wrote that "the whole world is in the power of the evil one" (1 John 5:19). But this is precisely the worship of the creature rather than the Creator (Rom. 1:25). Satan's sway is the sway of an impostor. His dominion over the world is a false dominion, and Christ had come to take what was rightfully his and to restore the worship of the Creator.

In this temptation, as we have said, Satan was proposing an apparently simple and congenial method for Christ to fulfill his mission—a method, if anything, simpler than turning stones into bread or descending from the pinnacle of the temple: just one little genuflection! The temptation was as subtle as it was enticing. For Christ to have bowed down before the devil would have been for him to subject himself to the devil as his superior. Doing this, he might have seemed to gain the world; but Satan would have gained him and with him the world also! The false god of this world would have become the false god of Christ also. And the world would have remained unredeemed.

Christ, however, remained constant in his determination not to be diverted from the way of the cross; and yet once more he repelled the tempter with the sword of the Spirit, saying, "Begone, Satan! for it is written, 'You shall worship the Lord your God and him only shall you serve' " (Matt. 4:10; Deut. 6:13). Thus for the third time he quoted from the Book of Deuteronomy with its wilderness setting, so appropriate to his own immediate situation. In this place Moses was warning the people of Israel against the temptation they would face, especially in times of material prosperity, to forget the Lord their God and to go after other gods and in doing so to give priority to *things* rather than to the Creator and his will. Satan has ensnared many by offering them *things* in exchange for their *persons.* It is always a bad bargain; and the same transaction was implicit in the proposal he made to Jesus: "All these *things* will I give you, if *you* will fall down and worship me." You get the things, Satan gets the person. Things for the person—these are the terms of exchange set by the devil. And the human tragedy is that throughout history men and women have madly rushed to sell themselves for the things of this world—worldly possessions, worldly power, worldly prestige, worldly pleasure. The consequence is spiritual bankruptcy, for in possessing them, the devil also possesses all that they have.

Our Lord, who had experienced the subtly magnetic force of the temptation to barter himself for things, was not speaking theoretically, but out of the depth of his own experience, when he said to his followers, "If any man would come after me, let him deny himself and take up his cross and follow me. . . . For what will it profit a man, if he gains the whole world and loses his own self? Or what shall a man give in exchange for himself?" (Matt. 16:24, 26). It is an altogether improper exchange. It is not only in primitive societies that idolatry is practised. In the sophisticated society of our day people worship money, sport, politics, and many other things, and what we worship we make our god, our idol. The worship of the creature, in whatever form, rather than the Creator is idolatrous worship. For Christ to have prostrated himself before Satan would have been for him to acknowledge Satan as his god—an act of apostasy from the one true God and the ruination of all that he had come to do. But Jesus, fortunately for us, sent the devil off with the peremptory command "Begone, Satan!" as he delivered his third sword thrust (Matt. 4:10). And so the devil left him; but it would be a mistake to suppose that he left him never to return and that that was the end of our Lord's conflict with temptation. As Luke says, the devil "departed from him until an opportune time" (Luke 4:13). He would return, and return repeatedly, to renew his attack on the incarnate Son of God, ever hoping that sooner or later the second Adam would be overcome, as the first had been, by the subtle force of his inducements.

The Return of Satan

The significance of the fact that Jesus was a man of prayer who felt the need and sought the supply of strengthening from above should not be overlooked. We read how "in the morning, a great while before day, he rose and went out to a lonely place, and there played" (Mark 1:35). Clearly, prayer was a necessity for him. Indeed, since he taught his disciples a daily prayer (Matt. 6:9ff.), it was a *daily* necessity (cf. Matt. 14:23; Luke 5:16; 6:12; 9:18, 28). The Gospels provide numerous examples of the intense prayerfulness of the incarnate Son's life. Had he not himself been constantly prayerful, the conviction with which he instructed his followers that "they ought always to pray and not lose heart" (Luke 18:1) would have been questionable. The explanation of this necessity for prayer in the daily experience of our Lord is that, having taken our nature to himself in the incarnation, day by day he was tempted just as we are tempted (Heb. 4:15) and needed power from above, just as we do, in order to gain the victory. The prayerfulness of Christ should not be dissociated from his constant conflict with temptation. By his example, he showed the importance of prayer for the overcoming of temptation and at the same time warned us, by implication, that a prayerless Christian will be a defeated Christian. One who was assailed with temptations, just as we are assailed, and for whom prayer was an indispensable means of strength was unmistakably one with us as our fellow human being.

There are, however, some specific occasions that show how the devil persisted in attempting to dissuade Jesus or turn him aside from going to Calvary and thus to thwart the whole purpose of the incarnation. One such attempt was made soon after Peter's confession of Jesus as "the Christ, the Son of the living God" at Caesarea Philippi (Matt. 16:16). Matthew records that "from that time Jesus began to show his disciples that he must go to Jerusalem and suffer many things . . . and be killed, and on the third day be raised." The same apostle who had recently made the famous confession now vehemently rebuked Jesus, saying, "God forbid, Lord! This shall never happen to you"; but in speaking thus it was as though the devil was speaking through him, tempting Jesus once more to take an easier way. Hence our Lord's rejoinder to Peter: "Get behind me Satan! You are a hindrance to me; for you are not on the side of God, but of men" (Matt. 16:21–23). Peter undoubtedly meant well, but as yet he had no comprehension of the necessity of the cross and, despite Christ's clear instruction, could not envisage how his Master's kingdom was to be established by the way of crucifixion. Even when he and his fellow apostles perceived that the road Jesus was walking would lead to his death, it seemed like a lost cause to them, and they could but show their loyalty by expressing their willingness to suffer and die with him (Matt. 26:31–35; Mark 14:26–31; John 11:16; 13:37f.), though the event would prove that they lacked the strength to hold to this resolution (Matt. 26:56).

But afterwards, enlightened by the Holy Spirit, Peter had a full understanding of the Lord's teaching and proclaimed the central importance of the cross in the plan of God for our salvation, affirming that we were redeemed, "not with perishable things such as silver or gold, but with the precious blood of Christ, like that of a lamb without blemish or spot," and that Christ "died for sins once for all, the righteous for the unrighteous, that he might bring us to God" when he "bore our sins in his body on the tree" (1 Pet. 1:18f.; 3:18; 2:24).

If Satan could not turn Jesus aside from his set purpose of going to the cross, there might be the possibility of preventing him from reaching that destination by inciting those who were hostile to our Lord to put an end to his life prematurely. There are evidences of this tactical variation in the Gospels. When, for example, the members of the synagogue congregation in Nazareth, enraged by his teaching, "rose up and put him out of the city, and led him to the brow of the hill on which their city was built, that they might throw him down headlong." Luke laconically narrates that "passing through the midst of them he went away" (Luke 4:28–30). Later, in Jerusalem, officers who had been sent by the religious leaders to arrest Jesus surprisingly found themselves impotent to lay hands on him (John 7:32, 44–46); and not long after, when those who had been disputing with him took up stones to kill him, Jesus had the power to withdraw himself without suffering harm (John 8:59; see also 10:39). In these and other eventualities Jesus discerned the impulse of the devil attempting to do away with him and thus prevent him coming to Calvary.

Of particular significance in this connection was the consciousness of Jesus that he was purposefully moving on towards that *hour* for which he had come into the world, the hour of the cross. This was the goal he had constantly before him.

Only when his time had fully come would his opponents be able to lay violent hands upon him (John 7:8). It was because "his hour had not yet come" that Satan failed through their instrumentality to bring about his death (John 8:20). But when the time appointed for him to be lifted up on the cross for our redemption arrived, Jesus declared, "The hour has come for the Son of man to be glorified" (John 12:23). The moment for the fulfillment of his life-saving mission was at hand, and this was a moment of glory for him; but none the less, it was a time of bitter anguish and suffering for him. Hence his *cri de coeur* as he faced this supreme crisis: "Now is my soul troubled. And what shall I say, 'Father, save me from this hour'?" To this he immediately and resolutely responded, "For this purpose I have come to this hour" (John 12:27). It was his glorious hour, first, as he explained, because "now is the judgment of this world, now shall the ruler of this world be cast out" and, second, because "I, when I am lifted up from the earth, will draw all men to myself" (John 12:31f.). Coming to and embracing this hour meant his loving to the very end those who were in the world (John 13:1). This was to be the ultimate test and, as always, he prepared himself for it with prayer: "Father, the hour has come; glorify thy Son that the Son may glorify thee" (John 17:1).

The agony in the garden of Gethsemane must be seen as an integral part of that "hour" for which the Son came into our world, indeed as inseparable from the climactic temptation by which he was now assailed. There was the natural disinclination to pass through the dark and horrifying ordeal to which he had committed himself. He shrank back, certainly, from the dreadful physical torment and pain of the brutal humiliation and death now to be endured by him—not that he was altogether unique in this, for others had endured (and would endure with him) the same cruel manner of dying by crucifixion. But he, who had unfailingly given healing from pain and newness of life to the afflicted, would himself suffer more intensely than all others. The physical part of his suffering, however, intense though it was, was the least part of his pain and anguish. Infinitely more appalling was the deep reality of his spiritual suffering that involved the bearing of our sins and their punishment in our stead—in short, the actual enduring of our hell so that we might be exalted to his heaven. Unless we understand this, we will not truly understand his prayer in the garden: "My Father, if it be possible, let this cup pass from me; nevertheless, not as I will, but as thou wilt" (Matt. 26:39). Nor will we understand his cry of dereliction from the cross, "My God, my God, why hast thou forsaken me?" (Matt. 27:46)—the most dreadful cry of anguish that has ever rent the air, for it was the cry of the Son hell-stricken for us and isolated in the abyss of our dereliction.

No wonder the incarnate Son's sweat in the garden was "like great drops of blood falling down upon the ground" (Luke 22:44)! No wonder that he "offered up prayers and supplications, with loud cries and tears, to him who was able to save him from death" and who heard him because of his submissive spirit (Heb. 5:7)—to save him, that is, not from the experience of death but by raising him from the dead. Moreover, as we have indicated, the death from which he was raised was not merely the physical death of the body, which is the "first death," but also the spiritual death of the soul as well as the body, which is the "second death," the death of our damnation (see Matt. 10:28; Rev. 2:11; 20:6, 14; 21:8). How great was the temptation to avoid so unspeakable an ordeal! How amazing was the love and the constancy that caused him to bear it for us, especially when we consider that as the Son of God he is the life and light of all being and that as the incarnate Son he was entirely without sin and therefore owed no debt of death!

Plainly, the cross held no attraction for Christ, and, had there been a way for him to bypass it, he would have welcomed it. Through the agonizing at Gethsemane, his acceptance of the cross was sealed: it was from there he went to his trial and crucifixion. Should it be asked why some gentler, less harrowing form of dying would not have sufficed, the answer is that it was necessary for him to be *publicly* tried and condemned to death, for his innocence to be openly declared by his judge, and yet for the manner of his execution to be that prescribed for the lowest type of criminal and in the place of the guilty. It would not have done for him to have died privately at home or as the result of an accident or violent assault. His death on the cross prepared for Barabbas, a blood-guilty criminal, demonstrated the substitutionary truth of the atonement and declared that the grace of his cross reaches out even to the basest of sinners, so that the believer can confidently say, "By his wounds I have been healed" (1 Pet. 2:24)—an illusion to the teaching of Isaiah 53, the fulfillment of which is repeatedly assigned to Christ by the apostolic authors of the New Testament and, more particularly in this place, an allusion to verses 5 and 6 of that chapter, as follows: "He was wounded for our transgressions, he was bruised for our iniquities; upon him was the chastisement that made us whole, and with his stripes we are healed. All we like sheep have gone astray; we have turned every one to his own way; And the Lord has laid on him the iniquity of us all." There is no more classical statement of the significance and the effect of Christ's death on the cross.

In the garden of Gethsemane, Jesus wrestled agonizingly with the powerful temptation to abandon the whole project, and, having gained the victory, he went on to Calvary. But this did not mean that his battles with temptation were over. The cross itself was his ultimate trial and the concentration of all his testing. It was there that his being made perfect through suffering (Heb. 2:10) was consummated and there that through death he destroyed the devil who wielded the power of death (Heb. 2:14); for the cross was the fulfillment of the purpose of his coming and therefore his victory and his glory, contrary to all outward appearances. Yet even when Jesus was nailed in apparent helplessness on the cross, the devil perceived that there was still a possibility of tempting the incarnate Son to abort his saving action, and so he made one last desperate effort to bring him down to defeat. Certainly, the suffering, immobile figure on the cross was the picture of powerlessness; far from looking like one who could save others, he himself seemed in dire need of being saved. His crucifixion appeared to be the unquestionable contradiction of his claim to be the savior of the world, indeed the denial even of his power to save himself. The devil, however, knew better and so returned to the attack in a last-minute attempt to get Jesus off the cross and thus to snatch victory from the very jaws of defeat. He, who could have turned stones into bread in the wilderness or could have descended spectacularly from the pinnacle of the temple, could even, if he wished, save himself by coming down from the cross.

As Satan had on a previous occasion tempted Jesus through the lips of Simon Peter to turn aside from the cross, so now Satan tempted Jesus through the cruel taunts of those who were watching him and taking pleasure in derisively mocking his helplessness. Wagging their heads, they said, "You who would destroy the temple and build it in three days, save yourself! If you are the Son of God, come down from the cross." And again: "He saved others; he cannot save himself. He is the King of Israel; let him come down now from the cross, and we will believe in him. He trusts in God; let God deliver him now, if he desires him; for he said, 'I am the Son of God' " (Matt. 27:39–43). The voice was the voice of Satan, who in the wilderness had used the formula "If you are the Son of God" (Matt. 4:3, 6). There Satan had tempted Jesus to prove that he was the Son of God by performing a miracle and at the same time saving himself; and there, again, Satan had tempted Jesus to leap down unharmed in the sight of the people, who would then have flocked to him as their Messiah. Now, at this eleventh hour, Jesus was invited again to achieve the double benefit of saving himself and of convincing the people to believe in him by miraculously descending from the cross.

Least of all did he, nailed to that cross, look like the Son of God who had power to save either himself or others. Yet it was precisely that power that he possessed, and it was precisely the saving of others that he was accomplishing there. For Jesus was not really powerless; he could have come down, and had he done so it would beyond doubt have created a great sensation among the populace. They all would have followed him; but they would have remained unsaved, for the true victor would have been Satan, not Christ, whose goal, so nearly attained, would after all have been lost.

On that cross, Christ was not as helpless as he looked. Because it was of his own purpose and volition that he had submitted to crucifixion, his passivity at Calvary cannot be dissociated from his activity. It belonged to the intention of his coming, which was to give his life as a ransom for many (Mark 10:45). His acceptance of powerlessness belonged to his power. Hence his emphatic assertion "I lay down my life, that I may take it again. No one takes it from me, but I lay it down of my own accord. I have power to lay it down, and I have power to take it again" (John 10:17f.). He did not find the agony on the cross congenial. It would have been the most welcome relief to come down from the cross; and it was within his power to do so. Moreover, it would have silenced the denial by the mocking bystanders of his divine sonship and his ability to save himself. But, as we have said, it would also have

23

defeated the purpose of his incarnation. Yet it was a very real and enticing temptation that he faced and overcame in the midst of his suffering. The fact is that it took more power for him to continue hanging on the cross and to die there than it would have taken for him to release himself from that gibbet. The cross, then, was the climax and the concentration of all our Lord's temptations, and his death at Calvary, contrary to all appearances, was his absolute triumph over temptation and the source to us of eternal salvation. As he had taught his disciples that he would not only suffer and die but also rise on the third day from the dead, so his power was displayed and his victory sealed by his resurrection. And now as our ever-living Redeemer and Lord he makes available to us the power to gain the victory over the temptations by which we are daily assailed.

Overcoming Our Temptations

Perfect holiness of life was the essential preliminary to the death of Christ on the cross for us sinners. The perfection of his righteousness was established by his resolute endurance and unfailing conquest of all temptation. Only thus was he qualified to die "for sins once for all, the righteous for the unrighteous, that he might bring us to God" (1 Pet. 3:18). It is our unholiness and ungodliness that created our need of redemption, and it is the love and mercy of a holy God that provided that redemption through our Lord Jesus Christ. Obviously, God has not saved us from our unholiness in order that we should continue living unholy lives. The will of God for us is our sanctification; "for God has not called us for uncleanness, but in holiness" (1 Thess. 4:3, 7). Christ "bore our sins in his body on the tree, that we might die to sin and live to righteousness" (1 Pet. 2:24). This is the meaning of our baptism, which signifies dying to the old life of sin and rising to newness of life in Christ. Grace cancels sin, but sin does not generate grace. "Are we to continue in sin that grace may abound?" the Apostle asked (no doubt with reference to false notions that were gaining currency). And he answered emphatically, "By no means! How can we who died to sin still live in it?" (Rom. 6:1-4).

Another erroneous notion that needed to be corrected was that the Christian, freely justified by divine grace through the imputing of Christ's righteousness to him, was not at liberty to indulge without condemnation in all kinds of sin. "Are we to sin because we are not under law but under grace?" Paul asked again and with equal emphasis answered, "By no means! Do you not know that if you yield yourselves to any one as obedient slaves, you are slaves of the one whom you obey, either of sin, which leads to death, or of obedience, which leads to righteousness?" Hence the logic of the exhortation that follows: "For just as you once yielded our members to impurity and to greater and greater iniquity, so now yield your members to righteousness for sanctification" (Rom. 6:15f., 19). Though by the grace of God we are redeemed from the power, the guilt, and the pollution of sin, we still have to battle against the temptations to commit sin by which we are daily assailed. Strengthened by the Holy Spirit, we are enabled to follow the upward path of holiness. The alternative, which is certainly not an option for the Christian, is to consent to the impulses of the flesh; and to do that is to allow one's conduct to contradict one's profession. "Walk by the Spirit," Paul counsels, "and do not gratify the desires of the flesh. For the desires of the flesh are against the Spirit, and the desires of the Spirit are against the flesh; for these are opposed to each other." When we see things in their true perspective, we can but acknowledge that "those who belong to Christ Jesus have crucified the flesh with its passions and desires" (Gal. 5:16f., 24). Paul, clearly, was well aware of the reality and the strength of the temptations that Christians face. It was his own familiarity with the incessant activity of the devil that made him so concerned that those whom he had evangelized should remain firm in the faith. Thus, for example, he wrote to the members of the Thessalonian church, "I sent that I might know your faith, for fear that somehow the tempter had tempted you and that our labor would be in vain" (1 Thess. 3:5).

It is, we repeat, no sin to be tempted. To give in to temptation is sin. Every conquest of temptation is an advance in holiness. Temptation is an invitation to step downward and backward; but it is also an opportunity to step upward and forward. With the help of the Spirit of Holiness it can become a means of blessing. Hence James's declaration of the blessedness of the person who endures temptation (James 1:12)— endures it, that is, so as to overcome it. Moreover, as we shall show, there is an important connection between the temptation that we experience and the temptation that Christ experienced or, more particularly, between the victory he won and the victory it is possible for us to win in the conflict with temptation.

The objection is sometimes made that Christ, who never sinned, had less experience of the intense force of temptation than we sinners who have been beaten down and defeated by it; and, if this is so, the implication follows that he is less than adequately fitted to help us when we face temptation.

This argument, however, rests on a misconception of the realities of the situation. The fact is that because he alone unfailingly battled through to victory he alone has experienced the force of temptation to the full. Consequently, he knows far more about the malign power of temptation than any of us and is thereby qualified to help us in any and every critical situation.

The point is that Jesus was truly human in the way that we should be, but are not. In him alone the true potential of our human nature has been completely realized. To compare ourselves with him is to expose our abject failure to live our lives in conformity with the image of God in which we were created. While, however, he shows us humanity as it was meant to be, he also, through redeeming grace, shows it as in him it now can be. Only he who knew no sin could be made sin for us in order that we might be made the righteousness of God in him (2 Cor. 5:21). Accordingly, so long as this present pilgrimage continues we need to be "strong in the Lord" so that, having put on "the whole armor of God," we may be "able to stand against the wiles of the devil" (Eph. 6:10ff.).

We ourselves, as we know only too well, are losers in the battle with temptation, and , if Jesus had been a loser like us, he would have been of no practical help to us in this daily conflict. What we need is a winner, one who has proved himself through being completely victorious over the same temptations that we face. Christ's own personal endurance of temptation means not only that he fully understands the intensity of our struggle but also that, as the overcomer, now risen and glorified, he is able and at hand to help us when we are tempted (Heb. 2:18). Moreover, by his ascension he has opened the way for us into the heavenly sanctuary of God's presence, so that in his name we may confidently approach the throne of grace with our petitions for strength to enable us to overcome. This is very necessary for us, and it is something we are encouraged to do. "For," we read, "we have not a high priest who is unable to sympathize with our weaknesses, but one who in every respect has been tempted as we are, yet without sinning. Let us then with confidence draw near to the throne of grace, that we may receive mercy and find grace to help in time of need" (Heb. 4:15f.). He who on the cross bore the punishment of our sin has by his rising and ascension, and by the sending of the Holy Spirit, made available to us the power, the power of his overcoming, by which we are enabled to strive and to gain the victory. The Christian believer, "inwardly strengthened with might through his Spirit" (Eph. 3:16), can say with the Apostle, "I can do all things in him who strengthens me" (Phil. 4:13). Thus, though weak in myself I am assured of the total sufficiency of God's grace for every need (2 Cor. 12:9, Phil. 4:19).

In this connection the tearing in two, from top to bottom, of the curtain of the temple at the moment of Christ's death on the cross (Mark 15:37f.) had a special significance because of the truth it symbolized. This curtain, which blocked the entry into the holy of holies, the inner sanctuary of God's glorious presence, effectively indicated the exclusion of the people, because of their sinfulness, from that sanctuary. Once a year, on the Day of Atonement, the high priest, taking the blood of atonement from the altar of sacrifice in the courtyard, entered the tabernacle in the wilderness and passed through the curtain into the holy of holies, and there he sprinkled the blood on the mercy seat as an atonement for the sins of the people (Lev. 16). The populace, forbidden to draw near, watched expectantly for their high priest to reappear and for his announcement that the atoning ritual had been fulfilled. Later on, this annual procedure was observed in the temple at Jerusalem. But, as we learn from the Epistle to the Hebrews, the earthly sanctuary of the Old Testament was "a copy and shadow of the heavenly sanctuary" (Heb. 8:5): it was not the reality; it did not effect (except by anticipation) the truth that it symbolized. The endless succession of priests and the endless repetition of the sacrifices they offered indicated this. They aroused the desire, and pointed to the need, for the coming of the one great high priest who would offer the one perfect sacrifice for the sins of the world.

But the symbolism of the ancient system prepared the way for the coming of him who would be the mediator of the new covenant. It taught the important lesson that our sinfulness excludes us from the presence of God and that the atonement for our sins is effected through the shedding of the blood of an innocent victim in the sinners' place. The repetitiveness of the levitical sacrifices is explained by the fact that "it is impossible that the blood of bulls and goats should take away sins" (Heb. 10:4)—impossible because brute beasts can never be a proper substitute for human beings who are formed in the image of God. The reality portended by these "shadows" of old was actualized through the incarnation of the Son who, as our ever-living High Priest after the order of Melchizedek, possesses an eternal and intransmissible priesthood; who, victorious over every temptation, qualified himself to be the innocent victim; and who, by his partaking of our human nature (Heb. 2:14), constituted himself an authentic substitute for sinners, man for man. This truth is finely conveyed in John Henry Newman's verses:

O loving wisdom of our God!
  When all was sin and shame,
A second Adam to the fight
And to the rescue came.

O wisest love! that flesh and blood,
  Which did in Adam fail,
Should strive afresh against the foe,
Should strive and should prevail.

O generous love! that He who smote
  In Man for man the foe,
The double agony in Man
For man should undergo.

For the levitical priests there was no cessation from the offering of sacrifices; their work was never done. In contrast to this, Christ's sacrificial work as our priest was completed by the offering up of himself as the one sacrifice for sins forever, a sacrifice never to be repeated because it is all-sufficient for all persons and for all time. This contrast is brought out by the writer of the Epistle to the Hebrews as he depicts the priests of the old order *standing daily* in the execution of their sacerdotal office, whereas when the incarnate Son "had made purification for sins, he *sat down* at the right hand of the Majesty on high," that is, enthroned on high (Heb. 1:3). Every levitical priest, he says, "stands daily at his service, offering repeatedly the same sacrifices, which can never take away sins. But when Christ had offered for all time a single sacrifice for sins, he sat down at the right hand of God . . . for by a single offering he has perfected for all time those who are sanctified" (Heb. 10:11f., 14; cf. Ps. 110:1, 4).

On the basis, then, of the finished work of Christ, who offered up himself in our stead on the altar of the cross, and knowing that he is our risen, ascended, and glorified Lord, who has opened the way for us into the true holy of holies of God's presence, we are invited constantly, and not least in the hour of temptation, to avail ourselves of this free access to our Heavenly Father:

> Therefore, brethren, since we have confidence to enter the sanctuary by the blood of Jesus, by the new and living way which he opened for us through the curtain, that is, through his flesh, and since we have a great priest over the house of God, let us draw near with a true heart in full assurance of faith. (Heb. 10:19–22)

The Ascended Lord Our Intercessor

The description of Jesus as now *seated* does not imply that he is now inactive and does nothing further on our behalf. His priestly work of sacrifice, which was completed on the altar of the cross, is final and complete; it is never to be repeated, and there is nothing that can be added to it. But his priestly work of intercession continues in the heavenly sanctuary. Precisely because he is our ever-living Redeemer, he constantly supports and strengthens us with his intercession as we meet with temptation. Unlike the former priests who were many because "they were prevented by death from continuing in office," Christ is uniquely our priest without succession who "holds his priesthood permanently, because he continues for ever." Consequently, we are assured, "he is able for all time to save those who draw near to God through him, since he always lives to make intercession for them" (Heb. 7:23–25). The finished work of Christ on the cross is the foundation of his present work as our Intercessor. From the altar of the cross in the courtyard of our world, "Christ has entered, not into a sanctuary made with hands, a copy of the true one, but into heaven itself, now to appear in the presence of God on our behalf" (Heb. 9:24). Hence the first martyr, Stephen, in the hour of his supreme trial, "gazed into heaven and saw the glory of God, and Jesus standing at the right hand of God" sustaining him and welcoming him to that same glory (Acts 7:54ff.).

During the course of his earthly ministry the incarnate Son was accustomed to intercede for others. Thus when his own climactic ordeal was approaching, he said to Peter, "Simon, Simon, behold, Satan demanded to have you, that he might sift you like wheat, but I have prayed for you that your faith may not fail; and when you have turned again, strengthen your brethren" (Luke 22:31f.). And in the profoundly sacred prayer he uttered in the upper room immediately prior to his arrest, we are permitted to overhear, as it were, his high priestly intercession for those whom the Father had given him and for all who would believe in him through their word (John 17:9ff.). Satan continues in his attempts to discredit believers and to tear them away from allegiance to the Savior. But, as Paul insisted, being "justified by faith we have peace with God" (Rom. 5:1) and "there is therefore now no condemnation for those who are in Christ Jesus" (Rom. 8:1). Satan does not relax his efforts as the relentless enemy and accuser of God's people; but to no avail, for in Christ we are secure. No one, not even the devil, shall snatch us out of his hand (John 10:28). Because it is God who justifies, no one, not even the devil, can bring any charge against God's elect. The foundation of our redemption is eternally secure: "It is Christ Jesus, who died, yes, who was raised from the dead, who is at the right hand of God, *who indeed intercedes for us*" (Rom. 8:33f.; emphasis added). Having ransomed us at such measureless cost, he is not going to let us go. Though we rightly despair of our weakness, we can never despair of his strength. It is that all-prevailing strength that he as our Intercessor in the heavenly sanctuary communicates to us, so that our faith may not fail and we, thus sustained, may be a help to others who are being sorely tested.

The function of the high priest as intercessor was represented with striking symbolism by the "stones of remembrance" that were an integral part of the vestment known as the ephod made for Aaron, the first of Israel's high priests under the Mosaic covenant. The two shoulder-pieces of the ephod were set with two onyx stones, one on either side, on which were engraved the names of the sons of Israel, six on each stone; and on entering the sanctuary Aaron bore these names "before the LORD upon his two shoulders for remembrance." But the ephod also had a breastpiece in which were set twelve precious stones in four rows of three, on which the twelve names were engraved, one name to each stone, and for the same intercessory purpose. The instruction was given "So Aaron shall bear the names of the sons of Israel in the breastpiece of judgment upon his heart, when he goes into the holy place, to bring them to continual remembrance before the LORD" (Exod. 28:5–29). In this way the truth was foreshadowed that the incarnate Son, who is our High Priest and who knows his own by name (John 10:3, 14), bears us by name upon his shoulders, the place of strength, and upon his heart, the place of love, as our Intercessor within the heavenly sanctuary. It is by his strength and in his love that we are able to stand firm and to gain the victory in the time of temptation.

And his interceding for us is our constant need, because none of us loves God, as we are commanded, with all our being and our neighbor as ourselves. None of us is free from sin and failure. Indeed, "if we say we have no sin, we deceive ourselves, and the truth is not in us." But, "if we confess our sins, God is faithful and just, and will forgive our sins and cleanse us from all unrighteousness," assured, as we are, that "the blood of Jesus his Son cleanses us from all sin" (1 John 1:7-9). Accordingly, the Christian who suffers defeat and falls into sin still finds forgiveness through that blood of the cross through which alone there is forgiveness and absolution from all sin, past, present, and future—not that sinning is in any way to be tolerated or condoned, but because this is the true and all-sufficient purgatory that God has provided for us. The Christian believer abhors sin and strives after holiness, knowing that the will of God is his sanctification (cf. Heb. 12:14; 1 Thess. 4:3). He does not take pleasure in sin and is cast down by his failures. But when he does suffer defeat he is encouraged immediately to avail himself of the free access to the throne of grace that the ascended Lord, still bearing the scars of his atoning death, has opened up for him. His Advocate interceding for him by name in the heavenly sanctuary is the constant source of reconciliation. Thus John addressed his readers as follows: "My little children, I am writing this to you so that you may not sin; but if any one does sin, we have an advocate with the Father, Jesus Christ the righteous; and he is the propitiation for our sins" (1 John 2:1f.).

In a word, it is by faith that the Christian stands firm (Rom. 11:20; 2 Cor. 1:24). To imagine proudly that one can overcome temptation by one's own power and ability is to court disaster. "Therefore," Paul warns, "let any one who thinks that he stands take heed lest he fail" (1 Cor. 10:12). On the other hand, it is a mistake to think that the temptations by which one is assailed are unique or else more intense than those faced by others. No temptation is too strong to be resisted with the help of divine grace. The tempter's power is but that of a creature.

God's power is always there to bring us through the darkest and most oppressive tunnel of temptation to the bright sunlight of victory. The help that flows to us from Christ is more than sufficient for the hour of our direst need because, as we have said before, he has faced the same temptations as assail us, experienced their intensity to the full, and unfailingly gained the victory in the humanity that he shares with us. This has made him our compassionate High Priest on whose strength and love we may ever depend. We may be confident, then, not only that "no temptation has overtaken us that is not common to man," but also that "God is faithful, and he will not let us be tempted beyond our strength, but with the temptation will also provide the way of escape, that we may be able to endure it" (1 Cor. 10:13).

Through Prayer to Victory

From the Day of Pentecost on, there was a quite spectacular increase in the number of Christian believers, and this was not at all pleasing to the religious authorities in Jerusalem who felt that their influence was threatened by the success of the gospel. Peter and John were the first to be arrested, and, arraigned before the Sanhedrin, they not only testified without hesitation that apart from faith in Jesus there was no salvation but also, when charged not to speak or teach at all in the name of Jesus, responded, "Whether it is right in the sight of God to listen to you rather than to God, you must judge; for we cannot but speak of what we have seen and heard." On this occasion they were released after being threatened with dire consequences if they did not keep silent (Acts 4:1–22). This was the first moment of crisis for the young church, and at the same time it presented a not inconsiderable temptation to cease proclaiming the Good News. The prospect of suffering and persecution is never attractive. What were Peter and John to do?

This is what they did: they went to their Christian friends, told them what had happened, and then "they lifted their voices together to God" in prayer. The substance of their prayer at this critical juncture is recorded by Luke (Acts 4:24ff.); and perhaps as interesting and as important as the substance is its structure. The first thing to be noticed is that they start with God. The continuation of their Christian witness was at stake. If we find ourselves in a comparable situation of stress or peril, our tendency is impulsively to start not with God but with ourselves—calling God's attention to our predicament and pleading for protection and safety. That, however, has all the marks of self-centeredness, not God-centeredness. It indicates that we have lost the sense of proportion and priority by which our attitudes, as Christians, should be regulated. The Apostles, in their prayer meeting, had evidently learned the lesson that the model prayer given them by the Lord clearly teaches, namely, to start, not with self, but with God; for, doing so, immediately things are seen in their true perspective.

Thus the Lord's Prayer starts with God: "Our Father, who art in heaven, hallowed be thy name, thy kingdom come, thy will be done." And this apostolic group did likewise as they prayed: "Sovereign Lord, who didst make the heaven and the earth and the sea and everything in them." God, the supreme Creator of all things, is sovereign in his lordship over our world and its affairs. To remember this, and to put it first, makes all the difference: instantly it cuts persecuting individuals and authorities, whose power had seemed so alarming and invulnerable, down to size. Before God they are as nothing and less than nothing (Isa. 40:17). The Christian can confidently say, "If God is for us, who is against us?" (Rom. 8:31), as he appropriates for himself the reassurance given by John in confrontation with the anti-Christian forces that threatened the Church in his day: "Little children, you are of God, and have overcome them; for he who is in you is greater than he who is in the world" (1 John 4:4). When therefore we are tempted in the face of opposition to be dispirited or overanxious it will be wise for us to follow this principle taught by the Lord and practiced by his Apostles, that in resorting to prayer we should start with God. The vertical perspective invariably reduces the horizontal, which otherwise can be so frightening, to its true dimension.

The next thing that was done in the offering of this prayer was to recall what Scripture has to say about the kind of situation in which they then found themselves. This was also corrective in a salutary manner, for there is always the inclination to think that the crisis or emergency that one faces is unique and without precedent. By reciting the opening verses of Psalm 2 they could assure themselves that their predicament was far from unique—and, indeed, far from extreme, for this passage describes, not just the officious opposition of the power group of a comparatively little-regarded people, but the arrogant and mutinous raging of this earth's potentates and nations against the Lord and his Anointed. And, being well acquainted with their Bible, they no doubt had in mind also how the psalmist went on to say, "He who sits in the heavens laughs; the LORD has them in derision." The defiance of the Creator by creatures, no matter how powerful and numerous they may appear to be in this world, is nothing short of ludicrous!

This apostolic group perceived, further, that the words of the psalmist applied with particular appropriateness to what had recently happened in the city of Jerusalem where they were then assembled. They themselves had witnessed how, to quote the language of their prayer, "truly in this city there were gathered together against thy holy servant Jesus, whom thou didst anoint, both Herod and Pontius Pilate, with the Gentiles and the peoples of Israel." The whole world had seemed to be mobilized to bring about the destruction of God's Anointed One, and Jesus himself seemed to have been overwhelmed and obliterated by the hostile force of these world powers. Believing all their hopes to be shattered, the disciples had given way to despair. With the death and burial of Jesus the victory of the enemy had seemed to be complete and final. But now they knew differently. Jesus was no longer dead but risen and exalted to the glory he had left to come to our world. The victory after all was totally his. The cross had been his place of conquest, not defeat. What he had repeatedly told them about the necessity of his being put to death in Jerusalem and rising again the third day they now understood. Jesus was indeed God's "holy servant" who, as Isaiah had prophesied centuries before, suffered and died as the world's sin-bearer. Now the disciples could gratefully profess, in the prophet's words, "He was wounded for our transgressions; he was bruised for our inquities; upon him was the chastisement that made us whole, and with his stripes we are healed," for "the LORD has laid on him the iniquity of us all" (Isa. 53:5f.). That is the true meaning of Christ's cross.

As we have already said, on the cross, despite all appearances to the contrary, Jesus was not suffering merely passively but was indeed actively laying down his life as the Good Shepherd for his sheep (John 10:11, 15, 17f.). There God, far from being immobilized, was actively and powerfully in Christ reconciling the world to himself (2 Cor. 5:19). The cross was the achievement, not the defeat, of the Creator's purposes for our redemption. It was the zenith, not the nadir, of his grace.

The realization of this truth explains the startlingly dramatic turn that the apostolic prayer then took. The world powers were gathered together against God's holy servant Jesus "to do . . ." what? Certainly to injure and destroy him. But that is not how the prayer continues: "to do," they asserted, "whatever thy hand and thy plan had predestined to take place." In other words, they were affirming with confidence their knowledge of the absolute sovereignty of Almighty God. Appearances at the human level no longer deceived them; for they now understood not only that God overrules even the most vicious deeds of sinful people but also that the cross fitted into his predetermined plan of salvation. In the light of this knowledge, the Apostles' predicament paled into insignificance. God was in full control. There was no reason for them to be intimidated by creaturely displeasure and threats of violence.

And there was no need for them to ask for protection or for ease and freedom from molestation. Their Master's way to victory had been the way of the cross, and his challenge to them was to take up their cross and to follow him. "A disciple," he had taught them, "is not above his teacher, nor a servant above his master; it is enough for the disciple to be like his teacher, and the servant like his master" (Matt. 10:24f., 38). And so now, remembering that all things, including all hostile forces, are under God's sovereign control and remembering the extreme cost at which their redemption had been purchased, as they continue their prayer they do not plead for relief but for the gift of courage to fulfill, undeterred, the ministry of the Good News that had been entrusted to them. Seeing all things in their right proportion, they are now at last ready to bring before God the situation in which they are placed. Thoughts of alarm and crisis and of ease and relief have been banished from their minds. No matter what the cost in terms of physical suffering, they are eager to resume and intensify their witness to the redeeming love of God in Christ Jesus. They have placed themselves in the hands of the Lord, and therefore all is well. They do not ask God to silence or to incapacitate the anti-Christian opposition, as at first they must have been tempted to ask. They who had previously fled for their lives and denied their Master no longer do so. Their concern is no longer for themselves but for the Lord and the glory of his name. With regard to their enemies, they do pray, "Lord, look upon their threats," but this is immediately followed by the intercession "and grant to thy servants to speak thy word with all boldness, while thou stretchest out thy hand to heal, and signs and wonders are performed through the name of thy holy servant Jesus." After all, it is not so much they who were at work but God who was at work through their witness, and that made all the difference in the world.

The outcome of this prayer meeting testifies to the power of prayer, especially when it is offered in conformity with the pattern taught by Christ himself. Such prayer leads to victory over the temptation to stop speaking out or to settle for some kind of weak compromise when threatened with hardship and suffering. We read (Acts 4:31) that "when they had prayed, the place in which they were gathered together was shaken; and they were all filled with the Holy Spirit and spoke the word of God with boldness" and, further, that "with great power the apostles gave their testimony to the resurrection of the Lord Jesus, and great grace was upon them all" (v. 33). "Boldness" coupled with "great power" and "great grace" in bearing witness to the same saving truth is surely what is most urgently needed *in* our church today and then *by* our church in its witness to our nation and our world. We should pray, as G. K. Chesterton prayed: "Take not thy thunder from us, but take away our pride." The peace that we have in Christ passes all understanding because it is the peace of God, not peace from people who trouble and afflict us. For the Christian, tribulation and victory are friends, not enemies. Hence our Lord's words to his followers: "In me you have peace; in the world you have tribulation; but be of good cheer, I have overcome the world" (John 16:33).

The Necessity of Prayer

Nothing demonstrates the imperative importance of prayer more clearly than the fact that for the incarnate Son himself prayer was constantly necessary in his daily conflict with the forces of evil. Prayer was not only his direct line of union and communion with the Father, it was also a source of power and constancy as he faced temptation and opposition. If prayer was a necessity for him in his fellow humanity with us, how can it not be for us also an absolute necessity? Repeatedly we read in the Gospels that he sought solitude in order to give himself without distraction to prayer. Mark, as we have noticed, tells us that "in the morning, a great while before day, he rose and went out to a lonely place, and there he prayed" (Mark 1:35), and Luke tells us that on another occasion "he went out into the hills to pray and all night he continued in prayer to God" (Luke 6:12), and John records, in a particularly sacred passage, the words of his high-priestly prayer as the hour of his arrest and persecution was about to strike (John 17:1ff.; see also Matt. 14:23; Luke 5:16; 9:18, 28). Moreover, his praying continued in the garden of Gethsemane and also on the cross. Jesus, then, was speaking of what he knew when he taught that we "ought always to pray and not lose heart" (Luke 18:1)—in other words, that there is no circumstance in life in which prayer is not necessary for us.

This was the point of the parable of the unjust judge that Luke introduces with this explanation. The resistance of this judge "who neither feared God nor regarded man" was broken down by the persistence of the importunate widow with her demand for vindication against her adversary. This, of course, does not imply that God, like the unjust judge, is less than willing to grant what is right and will be persuaded to do so only after being worn down by our pleading. The argument is, rather, a fortiori, that he who is the altogether righteous Judge will not fail to dispense justice and that our pleas to him persist on the basis of this assurance. "Will not God vindicate his elect, who cry to him day and night?" our Lord asked. The answer was obvious, and it is this conviction that encourages us to persevere confidently in prayer (Luke 18:1–8).

It is a principle that received dramatic confirmation in the actual encounter of Jesus with a woman who was a widow (as we may reasonably assume her to have been). She approached him with an urgent plea and showed herself unwilling to be persuaded that his attitude was anything but positive to her (Matt. 15:21–28; Mark 7:24–30). This woman's petition seemed simple enough, for all that she asked was that Jesus would heal her little daughter who was afflicted with an unclean spirit. She had heard, no doubt, that he had healed many who were similarly distressed. But her earnest prayer seemed to stir in him no chord of compassion and even to be met with hostility. Being a Canaanite or Syrophoenician by birth, she was in Jewish eyes a foreigner, and the incident occurred in the region of Tyre and Sidon, which was her home territory. It is, in fact, the only occasion on which Jesus is recorded as having set foot on gentile soil. To this troubled woman it must have seemed like a God-given opportunity for her to obtain the help she so desperately desired, and so she called upon Jesus to have mercy on her and to grant healing for her daughter. But instead of receiving the immediate and favorable response for which she looked, her prayer, and the trust that prompted it, met with three severe trials, each of which could have been interpreted as a heartless rebuff and indeed a contradiction of all that she had heard of him.

The first trial was that her prayer was met by silence: Jesus "answered her *not a word*." What else could it mean but that he was unsympathetic and had neither ear nor time for her petition? Certainly, it is a trial well known to most Christians; for often, when blessing or enlightenment is most pressingly sought, prayer seems to remain unanswered. Instead of a word, there is silence. The heavens seem to be as impenetrable as brass, and God seems to be unheeding and unconcerned. The temptation is to conclude that he really has no interest in us and our problems, though we know full well that he is our heavenly Father who so loved us as to deliver up his only Son for our redemption and has promised to provide for our every need (John 3:16; Matt. 6:25ff.; Phil. 4:19). Such silences are intended to intensify, not to diminish or destroy, our dependence on him. But this woman was an outsider, and the disciples were quick to decide that she had no claim on the Master, indeed that she was just a nuisance to be got rid of. They interpreted his silence as meaning that he had nothing to offer her and did not wish to be bothered with her clamor. And so they demanded that she should be unceremoniously sent off. How wrong they were! It was actually they who had an important lesson to learn from her, not she from them; for on this occasion it was she, not they, who penetrated to the true mind and heart of Jesus.

Silence, after all, can be interpreted as ambivalent. Why should it be treated as negative? Silence says nothing: it no more says no than it says yes. If it is true that Jesus did not say yes, it is also true that he did not say no. Why then treat his silence as negative when it can with equal justice be treated as positive—indeed, with more justice, since it was his custom to respond with grace and power to all who came to him for help and healing (see the passage immediately following,

Matt. 15:29ff.; Mark 7:31ff.) And so the woman refused to take his silence as meaning no but decided that, on the contrary, it indicated that the door, far from being closed, was still open. Accordingly, she persevered with her prayer. Moreover, the fact that, despite the demand of the disciples, Jesus did *not* send her away was an encouragement to her to persevere.

The second trial tested the woman's trust still more severely, for, although Jesus now broke his silence, he did so in such a way that he excluded her, to all appearances, from the possibility of receiving the blessing she sought. "I was sent only to the lost sheep of the house of Israel," he said. This seemed to leave no place of acceptance for her, since she was not an Israelite. It looked like the cold shoulder of rejection. If silence was ambivalent, not so this utterance, which sounded like the exclusion of an unfeeling negative. Yet she was determined that he was not shutting her out. Though she was not of the house of Israel, she was a lost sheep, and he was the Good Shepherd who had come to seek and to save the lost (Luke 19:10) and indeed who had *other sheep* to bring into the fold, so that there should be one flock and one shepherd (John 10:14–16). He, uniquely, was the seed of Abraham in whom all the nations of the earth were to be blessed (Gen. 22:18; Gal. 3:16). And there had always been a place for the stranger in the house of Israel; hence the word spoken through Moses to the Israelites: "When a stranger sojourns with you in your land, you shall not do him wrong. The stranger who sojourns with you shall be to you as the native among you, and you shall love him as yourself, for you were strangers in the land of Egypt: I am the LORD your God" (Lev. 19:33f.). Women who were strangers, namely Rahab and Ruth, even had a place in the line that led up to the birth of the promised Messiah (Matt. 1:5). Such considerations, if they were known to her, would certainly have confirmed the rightness of her conviction that Jesus was not in fact shutting the door in her face.

In any case, she might well have asked what he was doing on her territory; for his presence there meant that he had come to her and that the coming, because it was *his*, could not but be positive and prompted by the grace and benevolence for which he was famous. Nothing could alter the fact that his presence was her opportunity. Had not the prophet proclaimed, "Seek the LORD while he may be found, call upon him while he is near" (Isa. 55:6)? His coming was the moment to be seized for seeking him, and his nearness for her calling upon him. She, however, forebore to argue, and she laid claim to no rights; all she did was to cast herself at Jesus' feet, uttering the simplest and most basic of all prayers: "Lord, help me." Doing this, she returned the ball, so to speak, to his court.

In the third trial of her faith, which now followed, Jesus seemed to show himself more harsh and hostile than ever, calling her, in effect, a dog, as though she were a worthless outcast. "It is not right," he said, "to take the children's bread and throw it to the dogs." Was he really slamming the door in her face? She at least did not understand his words to mean this but rather discerned that the door was still ajar, if only because the way lay open for her to be a dog and in that capacity to assert a right to have the scraps that fell from the Master's table. Thus she interpreted in a positive manner this apparently derogatory assertion of Jesus and by the persistence of her plea and the genuineness of her humility gained her request. She caught Jesus in his own net, so to speak—as he had all along intended and known that she would do—and won his commendation: "O woman, great is your faith! Be it done for you as you desire." Thus he showed that his true attitude had never been anything but positive and loving and compassionate. How could it be otherwise with him in whom all the promises of God are "Yes" (2 Cor. 1:20)? It is a truth that has been superbly captured in the beautiful words of the Prayer of Humble Access in Archbishop Cranmer's communion service: "We do not presume to come to this, thy table, O merciful Lord, trusting in our own righteousness, but in thy manifold and great mercies. We are not worthy so much as to gather up the crumbs under thy table. But thou art the same Lord whose property is always to have mercy." The importance of persevering in prayer, trusting steadfastly in the goodness of our heavenly Father, is often a hard lesson to learn, as the poet William Cowper discovered; hence the lines from his hymn:

> Ye fearful saints, fresh courage take;
> The clouds ye so much dread
> Are big with mercy and shall break
> In blessings on your head.

41

Judge not the Lord by feeble sense,
But trust him for his grace;
Behind a frowning providence
There hides a smiling face.

His purposes will ripen fast,
Unfolding every hour;
The bud may have a bitter taste,
But sweet will be the flower.

In a striking sermon on this passage, Martin Luther pointed out that, although Christ's statements to the Canaanite woman "seem outwardly rather a denial of help than room to hope," yet "in reality a promise was contained in them and hope rather than a denial—indeed nothing but a promise, though most deeply hidden and altogether secret under that silence and those answers, although they were hard, and a denial only sounded outwardly."

> These things show how our heart is wont to be affected in temptation [he continued]; for according as it feels in temptation, so Christ here behaves himself: it feels all things to be denied, when it is far otherwise. Therefore it is necessary that, leaving its own feeling, by a sure faith in the word of God it should conceive and hold fast the promise of help deeply hidden under the denial and yield to the sentence of God, as this woman did. So shall we overcome and take the Lord in his words, that he cannot but help us.*

"Lead Us Not into Temptation"

The petition in the Lord's Prayer requesting that our Father in heaven should not lead us into temptation has been perplexing to many. James teaches, as we have seen, that it is not God but our own desires that tempt us to sin (James 1:13f.). But the petition certainly envisages the possibility of God's leading us into temptation, and this seems to come close to our being tempted by God, even though it is the devil or our own lusts by which we are actually tempted. The explanation that "not into" is the equivalent of "out of," so that the petition means "lead us victoriously out of temptation," will not do

---

*Sermons on the Most Interesting Doctrines of the Gospel (James Duncan, London, 1830), p. 110.

because that makes it say exactly what the immediately following clause requests, "deliver us from evil," and it destroys the contrast between the two clauses (indicated by the conjunction *but*). To say "lead us out of temptation, but deliver us from evil" is not only tautologous, it is also incoherent.* The clue to the right understanding of this petition is to be found in the experience of Jesus himself, who, we are told, "was led up by the Spirit into the wilderness to be tempted by the devil" (Matt. 4:1; Mark 1:12; Luke 4:1). This terrible confrontation with the Evil One in our human nature, which the incarnate Son had taken to himself, tested him to the uttermost. It was an ordeal that we, left to our own resources, could not hope to survive and into which we should pray not to be led. Not only then, but constantly, as we have shown, our Lord faced and victoriously overcame the full force of evil, by which we have been defeated, and not least in his agonizing struggle at Gethsemane. It was in that garden that he urged his disciples, "Pray that you may not enter into temptation; the spirit indeed is willing, but the flesh is weak" (Mark 14:38).

Even though redeemed, our flesh is still weak and vulnerable. He, and he alone, has conquered evil. It was his compassionate awareness of our human frailty ("for we have not a high priest who is unable to sympathize with our weaknesses, but one who in every respect has been tempted as we are, yet without sinning" [Heb. 4:15]) that lies behind his instruction to his disciples to pray the Father not to lead them, as he was led, into temptation. Not that the Christian is left to his own resources, for he is promised the aid and power of the Holy Spirit in his struggle with temptation. Hence Paul's admonition to the members of the Galatian church to "walk by the Spirit" and not to "gratify the desires of the flesh," since the Spirit and the desires of the flesh are in conflict with each other. He reminds them, further, that "those who belong to Christ Jesus have crucified the flesh with its passions and desires." Nothing could be more logical and more necessary than that we who

---

*C. C. Torrey, in accordance with his thesis that all four Gospels are a Greek translation from an original Semitic text, contended that his method of retro-translation (which can hardly fail to be questionable) showed that the original had been misrendered and had simply stated "let us not yield to temptation"; *The Four Gospels: A New Translation* (London, Hodder and Stoughton, n.d.), pp. ix, 12, 292.

live by the Spirit should also walk by the Spirit (Gal. 5:16–25). To be tempted, we repeat, is to be *tested*, and the Christian should always regard temptation as testing. The lust of the flesh and worldly allurements are a test of his holiness, and persecution for Jesus' sake is a test of his constancy and his devotion to his Redeemer. Understood in this light, temptations can be saluted as milestones on the road that leads to blessedness. Testing can be transformed by grace into beatitude, as our Lord taught: "Blessed are you when men revile you and persecute you and utter all kinds of evil against you falsely on my account. Rejoice and be glad, for your reward is great in heaven" (Matt. 5:11f.). So, too, Peter, after speaking of the Christian's living hope and imperishable inheritance, writes "In this you rejoice, though now for a little while you may have to suffer various trials,* so that the genuineness of your faith, more precious than gold which though perishable is tested by fire, may redound to praise and glory and honor at the revelation of Jesus Christ" (1 Pet. 1:6f.).

In asking our Father in heaven not to lead us into temptation, then, we are not asking him to keep us free from all temptation, for temptations are inseparable from our present pilgrimage to the glory that is yet to be revealed (Rom. 8:18); hence the need for the additional petition to be delivered from evil. Moreover, we have the assurance that "the Lord knows how to rescue the godly from trial**" (2 Pet. 2:9), that we will not be tempted beyond our strength, that is, as believers fortified by grace, and that with every temptation he will provide a way of escape for us (1 Cor. 10:13).

We must distinguish, further, between temptations to commit sin, which test our faithfulness and must always be resisted, and trials that are morally neutral, such as persecution or a personal disability. The former are overcome by saying no; the latter by enduring them without complaint or bitterness, though the latter also come upon us as temptations to be resisted insofar as they incline us to abandon the struggle and deny the faith or to indulge in self-pity and to speak against God as though he were not our heavenly Father. It will be

---

*The same word in Greek as *temptations, testings.*

**The same word again as *temptation* in Greek.

remembered that the critical need arose for Paul to learn how to gain the victory over this sort of testing. What exactly his "thorn in the flesh" was we do not know; but it was some affliction from which he would gladly have been freed because in one way or another it threatened to be incapacitating for his ministry. He described it, indeed, as "a messenger of Satan, to harass me," and he says that three times he besought the Lord to rid him of it. No doubt he had to resist the temptation to conclude that the Lord was unconcerned about his affliction, and it was probably not easy for him to learn that, instead of removing it, it was God's will for him to live with it and for it actually to become a means of blessing to him.

Paul found that God is able to transmute a distressing condition into something that is positively beneficial for spiritual life and ministry. The answer to his thrice-repeated petition was negative but not uncaringly or unfruitfully so. He had had experiences and revelations not ordinarily granted to human beings, and the presence of his "thorn in the flesh" served to keep him "from being too elated." It was an abiding reminder to him of his human frailty and finitude and therefore of his need to think humbly of himself. It helped to teach him daily the importance of depending not on his own ability and strength but solely and entirely on the grace and power of God. It became a blessing to him because it showed him that his very weakness was the opportunity for the manifestation of God's power, which indeed was magnified through his weakness. And so the Lord's response to his entreaty was the assurance that "my grace is sufficient for you, for my power is made perfect in weakness." And Paul's response to this assurance was: "I will all the more gladly boast of my weaknesses, that the power of Christ may rest upon me. For the sake of Christ, then, I am content with weaknesses, insults, hardships, persecutions, and calamities; for when I am weak, then I am strong" (2 Cor. 12:1–10). Thus even our infirmities can be beautiful by the radiant light of divine grace and can become a resource for glorifying the transcendent power of God.

In the whole history of human testing it would be difficult to imagine a trial more severe and more dramatic than that of Abraham on the occasion when God said to him, "Take your son, your only son Isaac, whom you love, and go up to the land of Moriah, and offer him there as a burnt offering upon one of the mountains of which I shall tell you" (Gen. 22:1f.). Humanly speaking, this command made absolutely no sense. Isaac was the son of the promise and at the time the sole and vital link in the line of covenant grace that was to lead up to Christ and the restoration of all things. Putting him to death would betoken the annulment of the promise, the failure of God's word, and the destruction of hope for Abraham. If ever a man was tempted to lapse into despair and unbelief and cynical rebellion, it was Abraham at this critical moment. Yet Abraham's faith stood firm. He refused to doubt the trustworthiness of God's promise. He was fully convinced that God's declared purpose could not come to nothing. "God will provide himself the lamb for a burnt offering, my son," he told Isaac; and God did precisely that (Gen. 22:7ff.). As Paul testifies, "no distrust made him waver concerning the promise of God, but he grew strong in his faith as he gave glory to God" (Rom. 4:20). Indeed, he was confident that, even if Isaac should be slain, God would reconnect the line of promise by raising him to life again. "He considered," the author of the Epistle to the Hebrews writes, "that God was able to raise him even from the dead; hence, figuratively speaking, he did receive him back" (Heb. 11:17–19). God, after all, had already, so to speak, raised Isaac from the deadness of Sarah's womb; how should he not be able also to raise him from the deadness of the tomb? And so Abraham overcame *by faith* (Heb. 11:17), for "the God in whom he believed is the God who gives life to the dead and calls into existence the things that do not exist" (Rom. 4:17; cf. 2 Cor. 1:9). Accordingly, the promise to Abraham was reaffirmed, that in his seed all the nations of the earth would be blessed (Gen. 22:18). Thus, too, our testing, no matter how severe, should be the triumph of our faith in the word and the grace of God.

We have seen that it is no sin to be tempted and that this is most self-evidently confirmed by the fact that Christ himself was tempted in the same way as we are, yet without sin (Heb. 4:15; 1 Pet. 2:22). Sin consists in acquiescing in and committing the evil to which we are incited by the temptation. Though the stimulus for temptation may come from outside, for example from something we read or hear, the temptation itself resides within the person. As James says, "Each person is tempted when he is lured and enticed by his own desire. Then

46

desire when it has conceived gives birth to sin; and sin when it is full-grown brings forth death" (James 1:14f.). The sin that is thus engendered is often expressed as an outward act such as theft or violence; but, the tenth commandment, which prohibits coveting what belongs to someone else, clearly shows that sin can take the form of an inward attitude or disposition. The deep root of sin, indeed, is the denial or suppression of the truth of our creation in the image of God and our unwillingness to acknowledge that the fulfillment of the potential of our authentic humanity is inseparable from self-conformity to that divine image of our constitution. It is this depth of sinfulness in our fallen nature that explains our need of divine redemption.

Jesus, we read, "knew all men and needed no one to bear witness of man, for he himself knew what was in man" (John 2:25). That is why his teaching on temptation and sin is so penetrating. Thus, in a striking manner, he declared that commandments that forbid the commission of outward sins like adultery and murder can be broken inwardly, without the performance of the outward act. A person who harbors anger or hatred against another is breaking the sixth commandment, he affirmed, and any one "who looks at a woman lustfully has already committed adultery with her in his heart" (Matt. 5:21ff., 27ff.). How then are we to differentiate between the temptation to hate and to lust and the sin of hating and lusting?

The answer to this problem, which the Christian faces every day, is that the temptation to hate or lust (or to do many other things that are wrong) must be fought and overcome with the help of God's grace, whereas sin consists in not resisting the temptation and allowing hatred or lust to settle in our hearts and thus to form a disposition within us. We are to be forgiving, even as the Lord has forgiven us (Col. 3:13; Matt. 18:21f.), and we are to be pure, even as the Lord is pure (1 John 3:3). The apostolic formula for being angry without sinning is not to let the sun go down on one's anger (Eph. 4:26). John teaches that "he who loves his brother abides in the light" but at the same time warns that he who hates his brother has been blinded by darkness (1 John 2:10f.). There is something seriously wrong with a Christian who has allowed himself to become soured and vindictive. The Christian life should be productive of the ninefold fruit of the Spirit, namely, love, joy, peace, patience, kindness, goodness, faithfulness, gentleness, and self-control (Gal. 5:22)—in a word, holiness, which should be the hallmark of the person who is indwelt by the Spirit of Holiness and who is therefore God's temple (1 Cor. 3:16f.; 6:19f.). The Christian believer is stamped, as it were, by the Holy Spirit as God's special possession. Unholiness is incongruous with the salvation he has received and contradicts the faith he professes. It is grievous inconsistency. Hence Paul's injunction: "Do not grieve the Holy Spirit of God, in whom you were sealed for the day of redemption" (Eph. 4:30).

By its very nature, sin is contrary to God and his holiness. It is anti-God. That is why John asserts categorically that "no one born of God commits sin; for," he explains, "God's nature abides in him, and he cannot sin because he is born of God" (1 John 3:9; cf. 5:18). To the same effect, and no less emphatic, is his insistence that no one who abides in Christ sins (1 John 3:6). This looks like a manifesto for the perfectionist who claims to live the Christian life without committing any sin. But this is clearly not John's intention, for he has also categorically asserted earlier in the same epistle that "if we say we have no sin, we deceive ourselves, and the truth is not in us" (1 John 1:8, 10). This, however, appears to leave us with a thoroughly paradoxical situation. How can one and the same person be a Christian believer who, "born of God," commits no sin and yet a falsifier who is self-deceived if he denies that he is a sinner?

The resolution of this problem requires the following considerations to be taken into account. Sin is the foreign factor in the life of the Christian; it has no rightful place there. Obviously, for the believer who has been delivered from sin to continue deliberately committing sin is preposterous, it makes no sense, it contradicts the saving power of the gospel. The Christian's standing before his Creator as a sinner who has been justified by grace is entirely in Christ Jesus the sinless One. His duty and his destiny is to be Christ-like, that is, positively holy, not only graciously forgiven but also victoriously free from sin. But in the present pilgrimage, as we have previously noticed, there is a conflict between flesh and Spirit (Gal. 5:17), as any honest analysis of ourselves reveals. It is a self-analysis graphically described by the Apostle Paul: "I know that nothing good dwells within me, that is, in my flesh. I can will what is right, but I cannot do it. For I do not do the good I want, but the evil I do not want is what I do" (Rom. 7:18f.). From this we see the difference between the believer and the unbeliever. The former does not delight in the practice of sin; his mind, renewed in Christ, is set against it. But the latter, by reason of his unregenerate nature, is set in the way of ungodliness and is a practitioner of sin.

In principle, then, the Christian does not commit sin, though in practice he still falls short of the glory of God. Accordingly, John, when writing to Christians, can say, on the one hand, that "no one born of God commits sin, for God's nature abides in him" and, on the other hand, that to claim to be without sin is to be self-deceived and untruthful. And hence the need that the Christian believer should be assured that "the blood of Jesus . . . cleanses us from all sin" and that "if we confess our sins, God is faithful and just, and will forgive our sins and cleanse us from all unrighteousness" (1 John 1:7-9). We may be confident, then, that it is here and now that the blood of Jesus cleanses from *all sin*, whether committed before or after baptism, for the Apostle was writing to baptized Christians.

The Significance of Our Baptism

To this twofold and quasi-paradoxical status of the Christian, namely, that he has done with sinning and yet that he is still not free from sinning, the two sacraments of the gospel bear graphic witness. As Augustine discerned long since, the sacramental element must in itself be appropriate to serve as the sign or symbol of the truth to which it testifies. Thus the water of Christian baptism is an appropriate indicator of the inward cleansing from sin effected by the blood of Christ, since water is itself daily used for the outward cleansing of our bodies. It is appropriate, further, for the purpose of depicting the death of the Christian to the old life of sin and his rising to newness of life with Christ, since submergence in water is death to us in everyday experience and emergence from water is deliverance from death. Thus the inner meaning of baptism is the cancellation, through the atoning death of Christ, of the condemnation under which the sinner stands and also the complete and absolute break with the old life of sinning implicit in the rising to newness of life in Christ.

It should not be thought, however, that the power of this radical transformation resides in the sacrament, as though grace were initiated or brought into being by sacramental action; for the grace of God is always prevenient grace. It is grace that provides the environment for the sacrament and is the whole power of the sacrament. Apart from the priority of grace, there is and can be no sacrament.

If the once-for-all administration of baptism (the "one baptism for the remission of sins" confessed in the creed) signifies the once-for-all renunciation of the old life of sin and commitment to the new life of holiness in Christ, the continually repeated administration of the Lord's Supper or eucharist signifies the believer's constant need, by reason of the imperfection of his likeness to Christ, of cleansing and forgiveness as well as strengthening and edification through the body and blood of his Redeemer and Lord. Thus the communicant is invited to *feed* on him and to do so in his heart, that is, spiritually, not carnally, and therefore by faith and always with thanksgiving.

The theology of baptism is firmly propounded by Paul where he tells the Christians in Colossae, "You were buried with Christ in baptism, in which you were also raised with him through faith in the working of God, who raised him from the dead." They had been "dead in trespasses," but God had made them "alive together with Christ, having forgiven us all our trespasses" (Col. 2:12f.). The theme is developed more fully in the letter he sent to the members of the church in Rome, and the teaching he gives is entirely consonant with that which is found in John's first letter. "How can we who died to sin still live in it?" Paul exclaims. It is altogether unthinkable that the practice of sin is in any way compatible with the life of the Christian believer; and it is our baptism that negates and absolutely rules out the monstrous notion that the two could ever go together.

"Do you not know," the Apostle asks (with a note of reproof because this is something every Christian should know), "that all of us who have been baptized into Christ Jesus were baptized into his death?" And he explains further that "we were buried therefore with him by baptism into death, so that as Christ was raised from the dead by the glory of the Father, we too might walk in newness of life." The logic is this, that "if we have been united with him in a death like his, we shall certainly be united with him in a resurrection like his" (Rom. 6:2–5). The likeness proclaimed by baptism is that of death-burial-resurrection. We are instructed by this sacrament, as by the visible word of the gospel, that the death of the incarnate Son on the cross in our place is the death of our old life with all its ungodliness and guilt and that, united by faith to him who has united our humanity to himself, we are reborn to live the glorious life of his resurrection, re-created, indeed, to be what God always intended us to be. It is a theme of which the Apostle never tires. "If any one is in Christ, he is a new creation," he declares; "the old has passed away, behold, the new has come" (2 Cor. 5:17). So also he reminds the Ephesian Christians that "we are God's workmanship, created in Christ Jesus for good works, which God prepared beforehand, that we should walk in them" (Eph. 2:10).

In the light of one's baptism, therefore, one should consider oneself "dead to sin and alive to God in Christ Jesus" (Rom. 6:11). This is a matter of spiritual realism, not mystical sentiment. The victorious new life is even now a reality for our humanity, which the Son took to himself in the incarnation. But the reality of our oneness with the crucified and exalted Savior has to be expressed in our lives as well as believed in our hearts. It has to be worked at. It demands application on our part and single-minded dedication. That is precisely what Paul means when he writes, "Work out your own salvation with fear and trembling." That he does not mean "work to obtain your own salvation" (which would smack of pelagian self-adequacy), but "put to work, or live out, the salvation you already possess," is evident from the assertion that immediately follows: "for God is at work in you, both to will and to work for his good pleasure" (Phil. 2:12f.).

The believer's security in Christ is not a passport for him to be careless or inactive, let alone to continue in sin. His is a position of solemn responsibility. Being *in* Christ, he is to be *like* Christ. His baptism sets the agenda for his life as a Christian. "Dead to sin and alive to God in Christ Jesus," he has but one way ahead of him that he must follow. The conclusion to which he is committed by his baptism is summed up in the apostolic exhortation "Let not sin therefore reign in your mortal bodies, to make you obey their passions. Do not yield your members to sin as instruments of wickedness, but yield yourselves to God as men who have been brought from death to life, and your members to God as instruments of righteousness" (Rom. 6:12–14).

Perhaps more than anything else, we as Christians are prone to forget that we have been baptized; whereas it ought to be a matter of binding importance for us, not least when we are being tempted to commit sin and dishonor our Redeemer, to *remember* that we have been baptized, that we belong to Christ, and that our desire should be, as our destiny will be, to be conformed to his likeness. We need to hear again and to heed the admonition preached by old Bishop Latimer:

> Our baptism is not only ordained for that cause, to know a Christian from a Turk or heathen, but it hath a further significations; it signifieth that we must wash away the old Adam, forsake and set aside all carnal lusts and desires, and put on Christ; receive him with a pure heart, and study to live and go forward in all goodness, according unto his will and commandment. . . . So let us ever consider, in what trouble and calamity soever we be, let us remember that we be baptized, that God hath promised to help us, to deliver us from all our sins and wickedness, to be our God. And again, let us consider our promise which we have made unto him, namely, that we will forsake sin, the devil, and all his crafts and illusions, and cleave unto God only: and so, by the remembrance of this, we shall be more ready and earnest to strive and fight against the devil.*

Strength through the Eucharist

We have said that the death-burial-resurrection symbolism of baptism declares our once-for-all abandonment of or death to the life of ungodliness and our rising to the new life of godliness in and with Christ and that the regular participation in the other gospel sacrament of the eucharist denotes and is intended to meet our ever-present need for strength if we are to fulfil the total commitment implicit in our baptism (and ratified at our confirmation). We propose now to consider just how the sacrament of Holy Communion strengthens us to overcome temptation and to make progress in our striving towards the goal of being like Christ. When Christ, at the time of his institution of the sacrament, said to his disciples, "Do this in remembrance of me" (1 Cor. 11:24f.), he certainly intended that our remembrance of him should be more than the mere recollection of one who belongs to the past. This is apparent from the form with which he invested the ordinance. A simple

---

*Hugh Latimer, *Sermons and Remains of Hugh Latimer* (Cambridge: Parker Society, 1845), pp. 133f. The quotation is from a sermon preached in 1553.

remembrance could have been entrusted to the pages of the history books. But this remembrance was specifically associated with the breaking of bread and the pouring out of wine and with the eating of the bread and the drinking of the wine. This association obviously had its own particular significance; and the explanatory words that accompanied the use of the bread and wine showed that this ordinance was anything but pointless. Thus when he took and broke the bread and gave it to his Apostles he said, "This is my body which is broken for you." And when he gave them the cup of wine to drink he said, "This cup is the new covenant in my blood," and then he added, "As often as you eat this bread and drink the cup, you proclaim the Lord's death until he comes" (1 Cor. 11:24–26).

The celebration of this sacrament is the proclamation of the Lord's death. The remembrance it incites is of his body broken and his blood shed for us on the cross. It is a dramatic pointer to that sacrifice offered once-for-all for us sinners to procure our redemption. By it our attention is firmly focused on the true heart of the gospel, our faith is confirmed, and we are strengthened to resist and overcome temptation. As the catechism teaches, the sacrament is a means by which we receive that inward and spiritual grace of which it is an outward and visible sign. Not that the eucharist is the only means of grace, for the reverent study of Holy Scripture is also a means of grace, as, too, are the teaching and the preaching of God's revealed truth, the hidden hours we devote to prayer and adoration, and our fellowship in faith and worship with fellow believers. But as an ordinance instituted by Christ himself, this sacrament is not to be neglected or despised by us, especially as its function is to concentrate our attention on Christ alone and on his cross as the source from which the river of divine grace flows freely and fully to us.

The Lord's Supper declares to us, just as our Lord himself declared, "unless you eat the flesh of the Son of man and drink his blood, you have no life in you" (John 6:53). It is plain from this same discourse that Christ did not mean that his flesh was to be eaten and his blood drunk in a physical or literalistic sense. For his flesh and blood were intact in his presence before those whom he was addressing, just as his flesh and blood were intact subsequently when he instituted the sacrament with the words "this is my body" and "this is my blood." His intention, then, was explained by his assurance that "he who comes to me shall not hunger, and he who believes in me shall never thirst" (John 6:35). That is to say, it is by coming to him in faith that we eat his flesh and drink his blood. Hence the emphasis in the administration of the eucharist on drawing near with faith and feeding on Christ in our hearts by faith. This means that it is by saving faith in Christ that we eat his flesh and drink his blood not only when we partake of the Holy Communion but also at all other times. "To what purpose do you make ready teeth and stomach?" Augustine pointedly asked, and then added, "Believe, and you have eaten already!"*

That the eucharist is not automatically and without discrimination a means of grace, that is, of eating Christ's flesh and drinking his blood, is clearly taught by Paul, who, because of the deeply solemn import of this sacrament, warns that "whoever . . . eats the bread or drinks the cup of the Lord in an unworthy manner will be guilty of profaning the body and blood of the Lord" (1 Cor. 11:27). To eat and drink unworthily is to do so without faith in Christ as one's Savior, without gratitude to God for the love and mercy manifested in Christ's dying for us on the cross, and without hearts filled with responsive love to God for so great a redemption and with good will to our fellow human beings. The sacrament is so sacred an ordinance because its concern is the ultimate issue of our eternal destiny. Therefore it must not be approached lightly, but with self-examination. To receive it unworthily is not to receive grace but to eat and drink our judgment and condemnation. Paul even wrote that, precisely as a result of partaking of the sacrament irresponsibly and uncaringly, many in Corinth were weak and ill and some indeed had died (1 Cor. 11:27–31). That is why eating and drinking in the heart by faith and with thanksgiving is so important.

Augustine made a careful distinction between the virtue of the sacrament and its outward and visible aspect. He insisted that it is the person "who eats within, not without, who eats in his heart, not who presses with his teeth," that truly feeds on Christ, and he admonished that the sacrament "is taken from the

---

*Augustine, *Tractate 25 on the Gospel of John*, §12.

Lord's table by some to life, by some to destruction."* The primary and proper purpose of the sacrament is that it should be a means of grace and strength to the recipient, but with this solemn qualification: to those who receive it in an ungodly fashion, it becomes a means of condemnation. Like the word of the gospel, of which it is the visible representation, it is never ineffective: far from being a source of grace and strength to those who scorn the holy truth to which it testifies, it judges them and is a ministration of death instead of life.

In saying this the emphasis is necessarily on individual faith and commitment; but the eucharist is misconceived if it is treated merely as the action of individualists, for the strength that Christian believers gain from it is greatly enhanced by the awareness that it is a sacrament of unity. This realization adds immensely to the benefit received from it. The principle is this, that though there are many members, yet all are members of the one body—a truth that is attested also by the sacrament of baptism, for as Paul says, "by one Spirit we were all baptized into one body" (1 Cor. 12:12f.). So also with regard to the eucharist, the Apostle describes participation in the cup of wine as "communion in the blood of Christ" and participation in the broken bread as "communion in the body of Christ"—and "communion" means fellowship in corporate unity. "Because there is one loaf," he says, "we who are many are one body, for we all partake of the same loaf" (1 Cor. 10:16f.).

Our oneness is expressed in the coming together of persons who share and profess the same faith, but it is rooted in the reality that all are *one in Christ Jesus* (Gal. 3:28). The Christian's whole standing is *in Christ,* and it follows that the individual believer is one with all other believers because they too are in Christ. Where before there was disunity and discord because of race or class or color, Christ Jesus is now "our peace" who came to "create in himself one new man" and to "reconcile us . . . to God in one body through the cross, thereby bringing the hostility to an end" (Eph. 2:14–16). *Through the cross:* that is the very heart of our redemption and therefore of our communion in Christ, our crucified and glorified Savior who still bears the marks of his crucifixion. It is the truth insistently

---

*Augustine, *Tractate 26 on the Gospel of John,* §§12,15.

proclaimed to us every time we join with other believers to be blessed by the grace of this holy sacrament.

Ironically enough, in ecumenical negotiations this sacrament of unity has become an embarrassing symbol of disunity. Even within the boundaries of one's own denomination, its unitary connotation is too often dissolved in an excess of individualistic sentiment. The common expression "making one's communion," for example, is thoroughly individualistic, as well as being questionable in other respects. Moreover, the symbolism of the one loaf has been lost through the virtually universal use of wafers, which, though they may facilitate distribution, are artificial and remote from the bread of everyday usage. The restoration of the one loaf would, in association with the principle of the one cup,* contribute to the recovery of the apostolic significance of the sacrament. It would also be a visible reminder (with periodical instruction in class and pulpit) that Christians are not isolated individuals but belong together in the one body and have the privilege of bearing one another's burdens and supporting the weaker members and those who are passing through severe trials.

---

*The use of more than one cup, as a measure of expediency in the case of large congregations, need not be seen as a violation of the one-cup principle.

The Noble Army of Martyrs

In the ancient hymn known as the Te Deum, "the noble army of martyrs" has a special place, together with "the glorious company of the apostles" and "the goodly fellowship of the prophets," among all those who praise the Lord God. The term *martyr* has from the early centuries been accepted as a designation of one who has suffered death rather than deny Christ and his gospel; but it is not beside the point to recall that in the Greek language (from which the word has come to us) *martyr* means simply "a witness." Certainly, those who have sealed their witness with their own life-blood should be thankfully remembered. They are a shining example to us, and we should seek grace, should we be similarly tested, to emulate their constancy. There is no more severe trial of the genuineness of our faith and no sorer temptation to renounce our allegiance to him who loved us and gave himself for us (Gal. 2:20) than to be faced with torture and death for his sake. Faithful Christian witness, however, is to be borne in living as well as in dying. That is to say, there is a martyrdom of life as well as a martyrdom of death.

To demonstrate that this is so, it is necessary only to turn to an incident in the Gospels. When the brothers James and John came to Jesus and desired the privilege of being granted positions of honor in the glory of his kingdom, they had as yet failed to comprehend the true nature of his kingdom. The response of Jesus indicated that the way to his glory was the way of self-denial and suffering. "Are you able to drink the cup that I drink, or to be baptized with the baptism with which I am baptized?" he asked them. And when they replied, "We are able," he said, "The cup that I drink you will drink; and with the baptism with which I am baptized, you will be baptized" (Mark 10:35ff.). This assertion could well have led

57

to the expectation that both James and John would suffer the death of martyrdom; but this would, in fact, prove to be the destiny of only one of the brothers. James, who was beheaded by Herod, was the first of the Apostles to shed his blood in a martyr's death (Acts 12:1ff.); whereas John did not meet with a violent death but lived on into old age and died peacefully in Ephesus.* Yet both were faithful unto death; both drank the Lord's cup and were baptized with his baptism; both endured hardship and persecution, John in a long life that included a time of exile on the island of Patmos and James in a life that was cruelly cut short.

In every age there have been sons and daughters of the Church who have dauntlessly suffered and died for the faith; yet, as there seems to be virtually no good thing that cannot be corrupted, even martyrdom has at times been abused by the actions of misguided persons. It did not take long for a notion to gain currency that the death of martyrdom, or the baptism of blood as it was called, ensured the forgiveness of all sins and immediate exaltation to glory, and this persuasion led some to seek martyrdom for themselves. In doing this they betrayed a defective understanding of the way of salvation. They overlooked the truth that it is the blood of Jesus, and his blood alone, that cleanses from all sin (1 John 1:7). Their trust was in themselves, and in particular in their own martyrdom, rather than in Christ. They allowed themselves to be diverted from grateful acceptance of God's all-sufficient grace to what was in effect a rash attempt at self-justification.

On the occasion of the martyrdom of Polycarp (ca. 155) a Phrygian named Quintus offered himself for execution but, on seeing the wild beasts, changed his mind. This incident elicited the comment "We do not praise those who deliver themselves up, since the gospel does not so teach us."** Some

---

*There is no good reason for rejecting the accounts of Irenaeus and Polycrates in the second century according to which John lived to a great age, especially as Irenaeus had known John's disciple Polycarp. A somewhat late tradition that both John and James suffered the death of martyrdom is probably based on a misunderstanding of Mark 10:39 or may be attributable to the confusion of the Apostle John with someone else of the same name.

**Letter of the Smyrnaeans on the Martyrdom of Polycarp 4.

forty years later Clement of Alexandria found it necessary to denounce this distortion of martyrdom into an act of self-immolation as foolhardy and irrational and indeed sub-Christian. He pointed out that Christ's counsel "When they persecute you in one town, flee to the next" (Matt. 10:23) meant that it was not wrong for Christians to take care of themselves, though at the same time it did not imply that persecution and death would or should be always avoided. Christ, Clement wrote, "wishes us to be neither the authors nor the abettors of any evil to anyone, whether to ourselves or to the persecutor and murderer." Furthermore, the person who presents himself for capture "becomes an accomplice in the crime of the persecutor"; while to "rush into the heart of dangers" and to seek death from a selfish love of glory is to be no more brave than are the wild beasts in the arena.* To do this is, to all intents and purposes, to lead oneself into temptation instead of leaving the disposal of one's life and the hour and manner of one's dying in the hands of the Lord.

There are many throughout the centuries whose faith has been tested and proved genuine in the crucible of persecution. In the pages that follow we shall attempt to display their authentic spiritual nobility by giving some account of the faithful witness, in life and in death, of a few of their number who by their conquest of temptation and cheerful endurance of sore trials have set us an inspiring example. If we start in the Old Testament, it is because the Church of Christ was there, too, as Hebrews 11, that great encomium of the triumphant faith of the Old Testament saints, plainly demonstrates.** With their gaze of faith they penetrated the mists of the future and greeted the fulfillment of the promises from afar, and with them we, who look back on the fulfillment of those promises in Christ, are one (Heb. 11:13, 39f.).

---

*Clement of Alexandria, *Miscellanies* iv, 10; vii, 11.

**Moses is said, in Heb. 11:26, to have "reckoned the reproach of Christ greater riches than the treasures of Egypt." Cf. also Acts 7:38, where Stephen speaks of "the congregation *(ekklesia)* in the wilderness," and the statement of the seventh of the Thirty-nine Articles of Religion, that "the Old Testament is not contrary to the New, for both in the Old and New Testament everlasting life is offered to mankind by Christ, who is the only Mediator between God and man, being both God and Man."

Joseph—"God Meant It for Good"

In the Old Testament there are many personages whose faith was tested and proved genuine by the endurance of severe affliction. One of the most notable was Joseph, the son of Jacob and Rachel, whose story is told in Genesis 37–50. His troubles started early. The antipathy of his ten older brothers was aroused because he dreamed dreams that envisaged their bowing down in submission before him, and when the opportunity presented itself they disposed of him by selling him as a slave to a caravan of Ishmaelites who carried him off southwards into Egypt. To be hated and betrayed by his own brothers, sold into slavery, and deported to a foreign country was undoubtedly an ordeal hard for this youth to bear and to understand, and he must have been tempted to conclude that God had forsaken him. The truth, however, was quite the contrary, for it is recorded that "the LORD was with Joseph." This, indeed, is the constant reality that sustained him in this and all the trials that still awaited him.

In Egypt, Joseph's fortunes seemed to improve when he was bought by Potiphar, one of Pharaoh's officials, who was so impressed with his efficiency and integrity that he entrusted him with the management of his household and all his affairs. But another seemingly catastrophic setback followed when the attempt was made by Potiphar's wife to persuade Joseph to commit adultery with her. It was a temptation he resisted, but his resolute refusal to break the law of God and to betray his master's trust was ill rewarded; the temptress, thwarted in her designs, falsely accused him of attempting to rape her and vengefully secured his humiliation and confinement in the king's prison.

Even in prison, however, his outstanding personal qualities and abilities won the admiration of the keeper, who after a while gave him wide responsibilities and authority over the other prisoners. We are assured again that even in this humiliation the Lord was with him. Hope of release from his unjust confinement stirred in Joseph's heart because of his correct interpretation of the dreams of two of his fellow prisoners, Pharaoh's chief baker and chief butler, the former of whom was beheaded and the latter restored to his position in the palace. The butler, however, neglected to speak to Pharaoh on Joseph's behalf as he had promised to do, until, after the passage of two more years, his memory was jolted by news of a dream experienced by Pharaoh that none of his wise men could interpret. Then at last he remembered the "young Hebrew" and told Pharaoh how he had accurately interpreted his and the baker's dreams in prison. Thereupon Joseph was summoned to appear before Pharaoh, who described his dream to him. Joseph, ascribing all his wisdom and understanding not to himself but to God, explained that the meaning was clear: Egypt was about to pass through two seven-year periods, the first of great plenty, the second of devastating famine.

Pharaoh, like Potiphar and the keeper of the prison before him, was profoundly impressed with Joseph's competence and lost no time in placing the administration of Egypt and its people under his control. Joseph was then thirty years of age. He had endured some dozen years of hardship and injustice, but now he was exalted to the position of highest dignity in the country he had entered as a slave. During the seven years of plenty he made provision for the lean years by establishing great reserves of grain. Stricken by the same famine and hearing that there was "corn in Egypt," the surrounding nations also came to Joseph, and amongst those who came were his brothers from the land of Israel. There in Egypt they prostrated themselves before him as the one on whom the survival of their family depended. And so the boyhood dreams of the brother they had rejected and sold into slavery more than twenty years previously were fulfilled.

When the moment came for Joseph to reveal his true identity to his brothers they were filled with guilt and confusion. But Joseph harbored no malice, and an emotional scene of reconciliation ensued as he assured them of his forgiveness and declared that God had sovereignly overruled the course of events in such a way as to bring blessing out of the evil they had done. "God sent me before you to preserve for you a remnant on earth," he told them. "So it was not you who sent me here, but God. . . . You meant evil against me, but God meant it for good." In all that happened to him Joseph was a remarkable and consistent example of godly sincerity, not only in overcoming the temptation to doubt or deny the divine goodness during the years when humbling setbacks and injustices threatened to overwhelm him, but also in thrusting aside the temptation to indulge in vindictive pride and arrogance after he had been exalted to a position of power and influence. Through every vicissitude his steady trust in the love and grace of God never faltered. The overruling hand of God in the history of Joseph is typical of the caring control with which God governs the destiny of all who are his and directs all things towards the fulfillment of his purposes of grace. To know this is to be invincibly strong when we suffer adversity that appears to destroy our witness and usefulness and tempts us to call in question the goodness of God.

The Maccabeans—"Of Whom the World Was Not Worthy"

The comment "of whom the world was not worthy" is made with reference to those men and women who in the centuries prior to the incarnation triumphed by faith over diabolical trials and brutal tortures. These, together with all God's devoted servants in subsequent generations, constitute the "great cloud of witnesses," faithful in life and in death, who surround us as in a great amphitheater and by their example testify to us that faith is the key to victory (Heb. 12:1). These witnesses, we are reminded, "were stoned, they were sawn in two, they were killed with the sword; they went about in skins of sheep and goats, destitute, afflicted, ill-treated—of whom the world was not worthy—wandering over deserts and mountains, and in dens and caves of the earth" (Heb. 11:37f.). This is the last part of a recital that celebrates the valiant endurance of those who by faith have prevailed against the onslaught of Satan. It is obvious that many scenes were flashing through the author's mind,* and one of these seems to have been the epic resistance of the Hebrew loyalists under the leadership of Judas Maccabeus against the tyranny of Antiochus Epiphanes in the second century B.C.**

Antiochus was king of Syria from 175 to 163 B.C., and during his reign he vigorously enforced a policy of hellenization aimed at the obliteration of the Jewish religion. Practices and customs foreign to Jewish beliefs were introduced, and there proved to be many even in Israel who were amenable to the

---

*For example, "who stopped the mouths of lions" (v. 33) recalls Daniel in the lion's den, and the assertion "they were stoned, they were sawn in two" (v. 37) calls to mind the tradition that Jeremiah and Isaiah suffered death, respectively, by these means.

**The story of the Maccabean resistance is recorded in 1 and 2 Maccabees of the Apocrypha.

demands of Antiochus. The traditional temple sacrifices were prohibited; heathen altars and idols were set up; swine and other unclean beasts were offered up; a pagan altar was placed on top of the altar of the Lord; and the penalty for disobedience to the king's sacrilegious decrees was death. Moreover, the scrolls of the Mosaic Law were torn up and burnt, and simply to possess a copy of the Law was a capital offense. "Yet," we are informed, "many in Israel found strength to resist. . . . They welcomed death rather than defile themselves and profane the holy covenant, and so they died" (1 Macc. 1:62–64 NEB).

Judas Maccabeus was one of the five sons of a priest named Mattathias, who publicly proclaimed his determination not to deviate one step from his ancestral faith. He showed his contempt for the king's decree by killing a fellow Jew who had stepped forward to offer sacrifice on the pagan altar and also one of the officers sent by Antiochus to enforce the new cult. After demolishing the pagan altar, he called on all who were zealous for the law and the covenant to follow him. He and his sons then took to the hills and gathered round them a company of freedom fighters. On his father's death, Judas assumed the leadership, and it was not long before his valiant deeds made him a legend in his own day; indeed, his daring feats were so successful, often achieved against armies that outnumbered his force many times over, that he gained a reputation for being virtually invincible. His band was inspired by his conviction that "it is better to die fighting than to look on while calamity overwhelms our people and the holy place" and his belief that "many can easily be overpowered by a few" since "it makes no difference to Heaven to save by many or by few" (cf. 1 Sam. 14:6). Finally, however, Judas himself fell in battle (161 B.C.), and the leadership was taken up by his brothers.

Eleazar, "one of the leading teachers of the law, a man of great age and distinguished bearing," was another heroic figure. When his persecutors tried to force him to transgress the Law he indignantly refused. Then, embarrassed by his venerable age and dignity, they offered him a chance of avoiding death by resorting to a subterfuge. But to this he replied, "Send me quickly to my grave. If I went through this pretense at my time of life, many of the young might believe that at the age of ninety Eleazar had turned apostate. If I practised deceit for the sake of a brief moment of life, I should lead them astray and bring stain and pollution on my old age. I might for the present avoid man's punishment, but, alive or dead, I shall never escape from the hand of the Almighty." And so he was dragged away and flogged to death (2 Macc. 6:18ff. NEB).

No less intrepid was the fortitude of a mother and her seven sons who likewise refused to save their lives by acquiescing in heathen observances or resorting to compromise, though they were in the presence of the king himself. Enraged by their avowal that they were ready to die rather than obey his commands, Antiochus ordered that the first son's tongue should be cut out and that he should be scalped and mutilated while his mother and brothers looked on, and then he had "this wreck of a man, still breathing," roasted in a pan heated for the purpose. Yet as they watched this inhuman spectacle, the mother and her sons encouraged each other to die nobly. "The Lord God is watching," they said, "and without doubt has compassion on us."

The next five brothers suffered the same cruel torture, and each died with expressions of confidence in God on his lips. "Better to be killed by men and cherish God's promise to raise us again. There will be no resurrection to life for you!" they said to the king and added, "Do not suppose you will escape the consequences of trying to fight against God." When the turn of the youngest brother came, the king promised the youth wealth and high honor if he would but abandon the faith of his fathers. But the king's blandishments were brushed aside, and so he urged the mother to use her powers of persuasion. This she did with these words, "My son, take pity on me. . . . Do not be afraid of this butcher; accept death and prove yourself worthy of your brothers, so that by God's mercy I may receive you back again along with them." The youngest brother was then treated with still greater brutality than the others; and so he too died, "putting his whole trust in the Lord." Then, last of all, after witnessing the torments of her sons, the mother was put to death (2 Macc. 7:1ff. NEB).

Horrifying though such excessive brutality is, it is by no means unmatched in the history of persecution. Of this the evidence is all too plentiful, including the evidence of our own supposedly enlightened age. The witness of the martyrs, however, has at all times been a joyful witness to the sufficiency of divine grace, a witness of victory in the midst of pain and indignity and solitariness, and a witness of gratitude for the privilege of being called to suffer for the sake of him who at infinite cost to himself redeemed them from perdition and restored meaning and purpose to their lives. Their example has never been one of despair and defeat. As the smashing of the jars held by Gideon's three hundred caused the light of the torches to blaze forth in the darkness, so the shattering of the earthen vessels of their bodies has enabled the treasure within to be gloriously revealed (Judg. 7:20; 2 Cor. 4:7ff.). Weak in themselves, the temptation to abandon the struggle has been great; but strong in the Lord, their very weakness has been the opportunity for the manifestation of his power (2 Cor. 12:9f.). The greater the test, the greater the triumph!

Polycarp—"If We Should Suffer for His Name's Sake Let Us Glorify Him"

At the time when Ignatius, bishop of Antioch, was on his way to be martyred in Rome (ca. A.D. 110) he passed through Smyrna and was able to enjoy fellowship there with Polycarp (ca. A.D. 69–155), the bishop of that city. Then, shortly afterwards, he wrote to Polycarp from Troas, exhorting him to "press forward in your course in the grace with which you are clothed" and to stand firm against teachers of strange doctrine, "as an anvil when it is smitten," knowing that "it is the part of a great athlete to receive blows and be victorious."* Polycarp was then about forty years of age and throughout a long life as well as in a violent death he did not disappoint the expectations of Ignatius.

In a letter that he sent, together with copies of the Ignatian correspondence, to the members of the Philippian church, Polycarp showed himself to be a champion of apostolic orthodoxy. "Whoever does not confess that Jesus Christ has come in the flesh is antichrist,"** he wrote. "And whoever does not confess the testimony of the cross is of the devil; and whoever perverts the oracles of the Lord to his own lusts and says that there is neither resurrection nor judgment,

---

*Ignatius, *To Polycarp* 1–3.

**1 John 4:2f., where John is combating the docetic denial of the incarnation.

that man is the firstborn of Satan."* He urged his readers to forsake false teachings and to "turn to the word which was delivered to us from the beginning."** While the spirit is willing, the flesh is weak; and so we should entreat the all-seeing God not to bring us into temptation;*** and we should "without ceasing hold fast by our hope and by the earnest of our righteousness, which is Jesus Christ, who took our sins in his own body on the tree, who did no sin . . . but for our sakes endured all things, that we might live in him." Then came this exhortation: "Let us then become imitators of his endurance; and if we should suffer for his name's sake let us glorify him."**** Polycarp, who as a young man had been a disciple of the apostle John, proved himself to be one who practised what he preached.

Polycarp in turn had his own disciples, and most distinguished of these was Irenaeus, who much later on, when bishop of Lyons, wrote of his vivid memories of Polycarp and not least of "the accounts which he gave of his association with John and with the others who had seen the Lord." Irenaeus recorded, further, that Polycarp, "when a very old man," had "gloriously and most nobly suffered martyrdom . . . having always taught the things which he had learned from the apostles, which also the church has handed down, and which alone are true."*****

An account of the martyrdom of Polycarp is given in a letter sent by the members of his diocese, "the Church of God which sojourns in Smyrna," to Philomelium, a town in Phrygia, "and to all the brotherhoods of the holy and universal Church sojourning in every place." They describe the death of Polycarp and his fellow sufferers as "an example of martyrdom which is conformable to the gospel." Such "nobleness and patient

---

*Irenaeus (*Against Heresies* III, iii, 4) relates that Polycarp called the heretic Marcion "the firstborn of Satan" when they happened to meet each other. Polycarp's language here is reminiscent of Phil. 3:18f.

**Jude 3; 1 Cor. 15:3f.

***Mt. 6:13; Mk. 14:38.

****1 Pet. 2:21-24. See Polycarp, *To the Philippians* 6-8.

*****Irenaeus, *Against Heresies* III, iii, 4.

endurance and loyalty to the Master" were displayed by the latter that, "when they were so torn by lashes that the structure of their flesh was visible even as far as the inward veins and arteries," yet "none of them uttered a cry or groan." It was as though "the Lord was standing by and conversing with them." The spectacle caused even the onlookers to weep. It did not deter the mob, however, from demanding the blood of Polycarp. "Away with the atheists!" they yelled. "Let search be made for Polycarp!"*

Though he himself was undismayed, the aged bishop yielded at first to the solicitations of his friends and withdrew to the shelter of a farm outside the city; but he refused the safety that could have been his had he continued to take fugitive action. On the arrival of his persecutors he presented himself and conversed with them, and he gave orders for food and drink to be set before them. His only request was that he might be permitted to pray without being molested; and, this being granted, "he stood up and prayed, being so full of the grace of God that for two hours he could not hold his peace, and those that heard him were amazed, and many repented that they had come against such a venerable old man."**

On his entry into the stadium a voice was heard, as though from heaven, saying, "Be strong, Polycarp, and play the man!" The proconsul urged him in vain to have respect to his age and spare himself by reviling Christ and swearing by the genius of Caesar—though he did consent to say, "Away with the atheists!" but in a sense, of course, exactly opposite to that intended by the proconsul. To further pressure he responded, "I have been Christ's servant for eighty-six years, and he has done me no wrong. How then can I blaspheme my King who saved me?" On being threatened with wild beasts he declared that "repentance from better to worse" was a change not permitted to Christians. The proconsul then hoped to frighten him by the prospect of being burnt alive. But Polycarp said, "You threaten that fire which burns for a season and after a little while is quenched; for you are ignorant of the fire of the future judgment and eternal punishment which is reserved for the ungodly."

---

*Letter of the Smyrneans on the Martyrdom of Polycarp 1–3.

**Ibid., 5–7.

Thereupon, with the mob clamoring for his burning, he was brought to the stake, and there he lifted up his eyes and prayed, "O Lord God Almighty, the Father of thy beloved and blessed Son Jesus Christ, through whom we have received the knowledge of thee, the God of angels and powers and of all creation and of the whole race of the righteous who live in thy presence, may I be received among these in thy presence this day as a rich and acceptable sacrifice." And to his prayer he added praise: "For this cause, yea and for all things, I praise thee, I bless thee, I glorify thee, through the eternal and heavenly High Priest Jesus Christ, thy beloved Son, through whom be glory to thee with him and the Holy Spirit now and evermore in the ages to come. Amen."

When the fire was lit, the flames curved around Polycarp "like the sail of a vessel filled by the wind" and at length, when it was seen that his body remained unburned, he was dispatched by the executioner with his dagger. So powerful was the impression made by his martyrdom that some feared that, if his body were handed over to the Christians, they would begin to worship him in place of Christ—"not knowing," the senders of this letter pointed out, "that it will be impossible for us either to forsake at any time the Christ who suffered for the salvation of the whole world of those who are saved—suffered, though faultless, for sinners—or to worship any other." They explained, further, that they worshiped Jesus Christ as the Son of God, whereas they worthily loved "the martyrs as disciples and imitators of the Lord because of their unsurpassed affection for their own King and Teacher."* To Renan's description of Polycarp as "ultraconservative," Bishop Lightfoot retorted that Polycarp's was "an age in which conservatism alone could save the Church."** If by conservatism is meant concern to maintain the dominical doctrine of the New Testament, this is true no less of our age and of every age of the Church.

John Chrysostom—"Glory to God for Everything!"

"Their weakness was turned to strength," we read in Hebrews 11:34 (NEB) concerning the men and women of faith who have

---

*Ibid., 9–17.

**J. B. Lightfoot, *The Apostolic Fathers II*, i, (London: Macmillan, 1889), p. 443. Bishop Lightfoot's translation has been followed (with slight exceptions).

preceded us. Indeed, as Paul had to learn, only in our weakness do we know the power of Christ (2 Cor. 12:9f.). And this is a lesson for all to learn, not just those persons who by nature tend to be timid and insecure but also those who have brilliant gifts or occupy positions of leadership and who consequently are tempted to trust in their own abilities. John Chrysostom (ca. A.D. 347–407), who was born in Antioch, was one such outstandingly talented person. Placed under the best teachers, he soon gave evidence of his remarkable gifts as an orator and while still a youth gained a reputation as a public advocate with the prospect of a brilliant career before him. But after an inward struggle against worldly ambition he dedicated himself to the sole service of Christ.

Chrysostom was one of the young men who pursued biblical studies in the famous school of Diodorus of Tarsus. For six years he contentedly participated in the rigorous discipline of learning and the ascetic conduct of this monastic institution situated on the mountain slopes outside Antioch. The intensity of his self-neglect, however, was the cause of permanent damage to his health and necessitated, if he was not to succumb to the debility induced by his privations, the return to his home in Antioch. The next step for him was that of ordination to the diaconate. Another six years passed before his reception of full orders. Because of his exceptional rhetorical gifts he was encouraged to concentrate on the ministry of preaching. He was then about forty years of age, and during the next twelve years his powerful preaching drew huge audiences in Antioch and made him famous in the Christian world. He was small in stature, but his preaching allowed no respect of persons; nor did the fact that he was far from robust physically inhibit the vigor of his prophetic ministry. On one occasion after an earthquake had shaken the city he rose from a sickbed and ascended the pulpit to calm the fears of the populace. The proclamation of God's word, he told his hearers, transmuted his sickness into health, and just as it was a famine for them not to hear God's word, so it was a famine for him not to speak it.*

Migne PG 50 (Paris: 1859), col. 713; cf. Jer. 20:8f. Another celebrated preacher, Girolamo Savonarola, when addressing his great congregation in fifteenth-century Florence, declared to the same effect, "When I am up here [in the pulpit] I am always well; and if out of the pulpit I could be as well as I am in it, I should always be well"; in R. Ridolfi, *The Life of Girolamo Savonarola* (Routledge and Kegan Paul, London: 1959), p. 134. The name *Chrysostom*, meaning "golden-mouthed," was given posthumously to John of Antioch as a tribute to his brilliance as a preacher.

The death of Nectarius, the patriarch of Constantinople, had fateful consequences for Chrysostom. The vacant archbishopric immediately became the focus of the most frenetic and unedifying ecclesiastical struggle for power and position. The leading churchman in the imperial capital had within his grasp the means of great authority and influence, especially if he could win the ear and favor of the emperor. In rank and prestige, he was not inferior to the noblest princes. He had the control of dazzling revenues and was the dispenser of coveted patronage. At the same time he could hardly hope to be free from the attentions of parasitic sycophants and agents of intrigue. The vacation of the see was the signal for place-seekers and influence peddlers and manipulators to get busy. Theophilus, the power-hungry patriarch of Alexandria, driven by a spirit of bitter rivalry, attempted to secure for himself a position of dominance by engaging in an unscrupulous scheme to ensure the election of one of his minions. His scheming, however, was circumvented by the worthier designs of those who, convinced that Chrysostom was the man to give the godly leadership that was needed, arranged for the unsuspecting and unambitious little presbyter of Antioch to be brought to Constantinople. There Theophilus, under threat of exposure of his crimes, was forced to abandon his own candidate and unwillingly to consecrate Chrysostom in the presence of the other bishops who had assembled for the election. But Theophilus, relentless in his hostility, did not abandon his plotting and his animosity. It was he who was behind a campaign to demolish Chrysostom's character by slander and falsehood and his person by violence.

Chrysostom's past, whatever his faults, was clear of scandal and his integrity was manifest to all. With humble diligence he persevered in his ministry to the citizens committed to his charge as their fearless preacher and faithful pastor. His zeal for the reform of church and society had a powerful impact on the life of Constantinople; but in 403, a mere five years after his consecration, Theophilus convened a synod ("the Synod of the Oak") at which Chrysostom was condemned *in absentia* on a lengthy list of ludicrous charges. Infuriated by the passing of a sentence of deposition and banishment, which the emperor had confirmed, the populace of the capital was in a mood for revolution. Chrysostom could easily have become the leader of a massive insurrection; but the violence of an uprising was contrary to his mind, and, quietly leaving the city, he allowed himself to be conducted to Bithynia under cover of darkness. That very night, however, an earthquake shook the city of Constantinople and the superstitious empress Eudoxia, disconcerted by what she took to be a sinister portent, acted to procure his immediate return.

With his customary energy Chrysostom resumed his episcopal and pastoral duties. But it was not long before he met with more trouble. The empress set up a silver statue of herself opposite the church of St. Sophia, and the pagan celebrations it attracted were an affront to the Christians worshiping in their cathedral. Never hesitant to speak out, Chrysostom ascended his pulpit on the day of the commemoration of the martyrdom of John the Baptist and pointedly proclaimed, "Again Herodias raves; again she is troubled; again she dances; and again she desires to receive John's head on a charger"—John now being an allusion by Chrysostom to himself.* Far from pleased with this riposte, and nettled by his forthright denunciations of the luxuries and intrigues of the court, Eudoxia took steps to have him removed for good. A synod of sorts was put together and passed sentence of degradation and dismissal on Chrysostom on the pretext that his resumption of the episcopal office in Constantinople was unauthorized and uncanonical. At Easter the thousands of Christians who had assembled to celebrate the Resurrection were scattered by military violence. Sacred places were profaned and sacred objects desecrated. Attempts were made on Chrysostom's life. Seeking the peace of church and city, he bade a prayerful farewell to his weeping friends and fellow workers and then with calmness and dignity went off into exile in the custody of soldiers, as though he were a common criminal. The city became a scene of rioting and fires, and many of those who indignantly objected to the shameful manner in which their patriarch had been treated were tortured and even put to death.

---

*This incident is narrated in the *Church History* (vi, 18) of Socrates Scholasticus, a citizen of Constantinople, who was about twenty-four years old when Chrysostom was driven out. This is sufficient reason for accepting it as authentic, against some who have questioned its factuality. That it was not Herodias but her daughter who danced is of little consequence for the point Chrysostom was making; he saw the two women of the Gospel account united in the person of Eudoxia.

The only complaint uttered by Chrysostom was that by being expelled without any kind of legal trial he had been shown greater severity than was customary for murderers, sorcerers, or adulterers. The place assigned for his exile was Cucusus, a bleak and inhospitable town in lower Armenia where he could be expected to perish unseen, if, as was just as likely, he did not perish *en route* at the hands of hostile bishops and monks or barbarian bandits or from sheer physical weakness. His was truly a journey to martyrdom.

The merciless journeying in the searing summer heat across the harsh Asian wastelands was made all the more unbearable by reason of the fever that racked his frail body and the coarse black bread softened in contaminated water on which he had perforce to depend for nourishment. The ordeal, interminable as it must have seemed to Chrysostom, lasted for many weeks until Cappadocian Caesarea, four hundred miles east of Constantinople, was reached. "You may understand what sufferings I endured on that long and cruel journey, most of which were sufficient to produce death," he wrote to his friend, the deaconess Olympias, who herself had been subjected to persecution following his banishment. He arrived in Caesarea in a state of extreme debility, afflicted with a burning fever, wasted by hardship and heat and sleeplessness, and in desperate need of a physician and medicine. No wonder he described himself as "well nigh a dead man" when he entered the city. There, however, he was welcomed with respect and affection by the Christian clergy and people, who with loving concern ministered to his needs—except for the bishop, Pharetrius, who had no intention of making things easy for him and whose murderous mob of monks terrified even the soldiers in charge of Chrysostom and were more greatly feared by the populace than the fierce hordes of Isaurian barbarians who were then terrorizing the district.

And so, still weak and fevered, Chrysostom was compelled to move again, at dead of night and doubly imperiled, on the final stage of his journey to Cucusus, one hundred miles further on. In the darkness, which they dared not relieve by the light of torches, the mule that was carrying him stumbled on the steep and stony track and threw him to the ground, nearly killing him. As there could be no thought of stopping, a companion dragged him along by the hand and they pressed on as best they could on foot through the hazards of the mountainous terrain. At last, after thirty agonizing days, the unprepossessing destination of Cucusus was attained. There Chrysostom managed to survive for some twelve months— and not merely to survive, for he who was no longer permitted to preach now ministered with his pen to those now far away and with his counsel to those who visited him.

Cucusus, in fact, so remote and unattractive in itself, became for much of the Christian world a focal point of attention. Adelphius, its bishop, received Chrysostom with honor, and the ailing patriarch was given the best possible care and accommodation. Friends and admirers even traversed long distances, as though on a pilgrimage, to spend some time in his presence. The pure air of this desolate spot actually seemed to effect an improvement in his health. The bishop of Rome, Innocent I, distressed and angered at the cruelty and injustice suffered by this saintly man, made an unsuccessful attempt to bring about his reinstatement. But with the approach of winter in the year 405, Cucusus, in imminent danger of being overrun by the Isaurian bandits, was deserted by most of its inhabitants, including Chrysostom, who with a few others found his way over the frozen heights to seek refuge in the comfortless fortress of Arabissus.

Here, he wrote to Innocent, he was "exposed to famine, pestilence, wars, continual sieges, indescribable solitude, daily death, and Isaurian swords," but "encouraged and comforted" by Innocent's confidence in the rightness of his cause and rejoicing in his "abundant and genuine love." Yet even in this inaccessible place (as it was understandably regarded) he was sought out by pilgrims, and he continued to wield his pen for the encouragement and strengthening of others. His freedom from despair and self-pity is altogether remarkable, and the intensity of his sufferings did not diminish but on the contrary contributed to the intensity of his faith. "Do you see the abundance of resource belonging to God—his wisdom, his extraordinary power, his lovingkindness and care?" he wrote to Olympias who was battling against despondency. "Therefore do not be dismayed or troubled, but continue to give thanks to God for all things." He gently admonished her that "dejection causes sickness" and that thankfulness is the antidote for this malady. Although in the eyes of the world he himself could not have been worse off, he considered himself to be better off than before. "Neither the inclemency of the climate," he declared, "nor the desolation of the region, nor the scarcity of provisions, nor confinement in one chamber as in a prison, and the impossibility of moving about which I always used continually to need, nor perpetual contact with fire and smoke, nor fear of robbers, nor anything else of this kind has got the better of me."* Chrysostom's secret was that he was not self-centered but Christ-centered. His true stature was his stature in Christ, for it was in Christ that he grasped the true proportion of his own situation: no suffering for Christ's sake was comparable to the suffering endured by the incarnate Son for his salvation.

Chrysostom's indomitable spirit and the joyfulness of his faith shone like a bright light from afar, to the embarrassment of his enemies whose embittered inhumanity was being exposed to the world by this one fragile, solitary, little old man. And so they took a further and still more drastic step to extinguish him and the brilliance of his witness. In the summer of 407, the order was given for him to be removed to Pityus, a town on the eastern shore of the Euxine (Black) Sea. The journey to this remote corner of the empire would have covered five or six hundred miles and would have taken a very long time. The two Praetorian soldiers in whose rough hands he was placed had been instructed to force him along relentlessly on foot, without regard for his age and feebleness. The country to be traversed was as harsh as the guards who were driving him on, unprotected against the sun's searing heat and through drenching storms. Undoubtedly, the intention was that he should be driven until he dropped and died; and this objective was achieved. The end came on 14 September 407 near Comana in Pontus. Utterly exhausted, the fever-racked patriarch breathed his last with these words on his lips: "Glory to God for everything!"

Thirty-one years later, by order of the emperor Theodosius II, Chrysostom's remains were brought back to Constantinople and interred in the Church of the Apostles. Not only his memory but also his teaching remained fresh in the minds of

---

*For Chrysostom's correspondence with Olympias and with Innocent I, see A Select Library of the Nicene and Post-Nicene Fathers, ed. Philip Schaff (Eerdmans, Grand Rapids, MI 1978; first published 1889), vol. 9, pp. 283–314; translated by W. R. W. Stephens, whose translation I have mainly followed.

the people to whom he had ministered so faithfully. His example of constancy and cheerfulness in suffering has ever since been an inspiration to succeeding generations. "I leap for joy," he had written, "as one who has a great treasure laid up in store for him," and he wished others "to glorify God who has counted me worthy to suffer such things." Thus all that he endured was overruled from above to bring about not an eclipse but an increase of blessing both for himself and for others. His last words, "Glory to God for everything!" are a fitting epitaph not merely of him who serenely died the death of a martyr but indeed of him whose whole life was lived as a witness to the truth and power of the gospel.

Henry Martyn—"Now Let Me Burn Out for God!"

No words could more accurately reveal the true spirit of Henry Martyn (1781–1812) than these, "Now let me burn out for God!" written by him in his diary on 17 May 1806, the day after his arrival in Calcutta as a missionary to the people of India. A mere half-dozen years later he would end his brief life at Tokat in Turkey, a town close by the place where Chrysostom had died nearly fourteen hundred years earlier. As we shall see, there was also a striking similarity in the manner of their dying.

Born in Truro, Cornwall, on 18 February 1781, Henry Martyn soon gave evidence of his brilliant intellectual endowments. At the age of sixteen he went up to St. John's College, Cambridge, and his career as a student was crowned by the distinction of graduating as Senior Wrangler, that is the top mathematical scholar, in an exceptionally brilliant field of candidates. There was no distinction more coveted and more admired at the university. With good reason, it was seen as opening the door to shining success in the academic or political world. The next year, Martyn was a prizeman in Latin and was made a fellow of St. John's College. It was during this time at Cambridge that he experienced a quiet but radical evangelical conversion that turned him away from ambition for worldly acclaim to the resolution to devote his life to the service of Christ and his gospel. In October 1803, he was ordained deacon in Ely Cathedral and commenced his ministry as a curate in the parish of Holy Trinity, Cambridge, under the celebrated Charles Simeon. The bond of friendship then forged between these two men remained close and unbroken throughout the remaining years of Henry Martyn's life. The disparity of age notwithstanding, each was profoundly influenced by the other. Both were men of culture and sensitivity as well as utterly dedicated to him who had called them to minister in his name. "Since I have known God in a saving manner," Martyn observed about this time, "painting, poetry, and music have had charms unknown to me before . . . for religion has refined my mind and made it susceptible of impressions from the sublime and beautiful. Oh how religion secures the heightened enjoyment of those pleasures which keep so many from God by their becoming a source of pride!"

In 1805 Martyn left England never to return. He had obtained passage on a troop ship in a large convoy of transports. The long voyage to India, which lasted for some nine months, took him via the Cape of Good Hope, then being annexed by British force of arms. Despite illness and discomfort and the crude antipathy of many of his shipmates, he daily ministered to the physical and spiritual needs of his fellow travelers and diligently maintained his own biblical and linguistic studies. At the beginning of that year he had written, "The same grace and longsuffering, the same wisdom and power, that have brought me so far will bring me on, though it be through fire and water, to a goodly heritage. I see no business in life but the work of Christ, neither do I desire any employment to all eternity but his service." As he looked ahead to his labors in a strange land he declared, "Oh, how gladly shall this base blood be shed, every drop of it, if India can but be benefited in one of her children," and again, "How happy and honoured am I in being *suffered* to be a missionary!"

Nothing was more uncongenial than idleness to this young clergyman, who even in college was known as "the man who never lost an hour." The conditions in which from now on he lived and worked were for the most part far from easy and commodious. Like Chrysostom, he was physically frail and constantly subject to bodily weakness. A congenital tubercular complaint rendered him particularly vulnerable to the extremes of climate that he would encounter in India and beyond. But his zeal was indefatigable. Difficulties and disappointments could not shake his confidence that in God's good time others would reap where he had sown, in accordance with Christ's own teaching (John 4:36–38). Every opportunity of proclaiming the word of God was eagerly seized, whether to the privileged members of British communities or to the troops in their barracks and on parade or to Indian citizens of the educated upper class or to the humblest inhabitants of the land; and he lovingly cared for the destitute and distressed.

With his exceptional gifts as a linguist and his delight in philology, he avidly studied and achieved mastery in new languages, in particular now Hindustani and Sanskrit, and also, with a deep inner anticipation of penetrating the vast expanses of Asia, Persian and Arabic. Proficiency in these languages enabled him not only to communicate with those whom he was trying to reach with the gospel but also to translate the Scriptures so that they could possess and study the word of God for themselves. Because of his expert knowledge of Hebrew and Greek, his biblical translations were made from the original text. In order to dispel at least in some measure the illiteracy that was widespread among the common people, he also took the initiative in setting up schools for children.

Martyn's exceptional qualities were not unnoticed by persons of perception. Sir John Malcolm, for instance, the distinguished author of a history of Persia, had the highest praise for his linguistic abilities. "His knowledge of Arabic is superior to that of any Englishman in India," he declared. And the Hon. Mountstuart Elphinstone, British Resident of Poona, paid tribute to his character and learning. "We have in Mr. Martyn an excellent scholar," he said, "and one of the mildest, cheerfullest, and pleasantest men I ever saw. . . . Mr. Martyn has proved a far better companion than I reckoned on, though my expectations were high. His zeal is unabated. . . . He is familiar with Greek and Latin, understands French and Italian, speaks Persian and Arabic, has translated the Scriptures into Hindustani, and is translating the Old Testament from Hebrew. He was an eminent mathematician even at Cambridge, and, what is of more consequence, he is a man of good sense and taste, and simple in his manners and character, and cheerful in his conversation."

The perpetual motion of Henry Martyn's mind was offset by the frailty of his bodily frame. This made the productive expenditure of his energy, physical as well as intellectual, all the more remarkable. His achievements, indeed, were truly phenomenal. Less than ten months after his arrival in India he had translated *The Book of Common Prayer* into Hindustani and was conducting services and preaching in that language.

It was said that he read grammars as other men read novels, and that to him they were more entertaining than novels. His unremitting application to the task of translating Holy Scripture was closely connected with his compassionate outreach to the multitudes living in spiritual darkness. He never accepted physical weakness and fatigue and constant illness as an excuse for inactivity. Other gifted men would have taken sixty years to do what he did in six; for it was not simply his gifts but even more his intensity—intensity in prayer and fasting and devotion to his Lord as well as in study and translation and preaching and ministry to others—by which his ability to compress a lifetime of work into a handful of years is explained. "I know of no parallel to these achievements of Henry Martyn's," a fellow missionary wrote. "Above all he prays, he lives 'in the Spirit,' and rises from his knees full of the mind of the Spirit. Pedantry is not in him, nor vulgarity. He longs and struggles to catch the dialect in which men may speak more worthily of the things of God. And so his work lives." It was his custom frequently to reread and privately reaffirm the solemn vows of his ordination. His intensity reproaches our lack of seriousness; it is an example to be emulated, not just a quality to be admired.

There is the well-known portrait of Henry Martyn that Charles Simeon received from Calcutta in 1812 just when his former curate was nearing the end of his earthly pilgrimage at Tokat in Turkey. It is a picture in which the eyes follow the observer no matter where he is standing. When the package was opened in London in Simeon's presence, it was a moment of deep emotion. "I could not bear to look upon it," Simeon said, "but turned away, covering my face, and, in spite of every effort to the contrary, crying aloud with anguish. . . . Shall I attempt to describe to you the veneration and the love with which I look at it? . . . In seeing how much he is worn, I am constrained to call to my relief the thought in whose service he has worn himself so much; and this reconciles me to the idea of weakness, of sickness, or even, if God were so to appoint, of death itself. . . . I behold in it all the mind of my beloved brother." Subsequently, when the portrait was hung in his dining room, Simeon would gaze at it and exclaim, "There, see that blessed man! What an expression of countenance! No one looks at me as he does; he never takes his eyes off me, and seems always to be saying, 'Be serious—be in earnest—don't trifle!'"*

Before the end of 1810, Martyn's body was so wasted by exertion and illness that his friends could hardly fail to regard him as a dying man. It was because he himself was well aware that his time might be short that he then determined to leave India for Persia so that he might preach Christ to the inhabitants of that country and of Arabia and provide them with the Scriptures in their own language. Yet he also retained some hope that he might be able to travel at last back to England and there be joined in marriage to his beloved Lydia Grenfell and then return with her as his partner in his missionary labors. But, as usual, he resolutely refused to allow personal desires and considerations to interfere in the main purpose of his life, which was summed up in his assertion "I wish to have my whole soul swallowed up in the will of God." Early in January 1811 he set sail from Calcutta, but with the intention, should God so direct, of returning after a time to his work in India. Daniel Corrie, another of Simeon's curates who had followed Henry Martyn to India in 1807 and who subsequently became the first bishop of Madras, wrote at this time, "His life is beyond all price to us. You know what a profound scholar he is, and all his acquirements are dedicated to the service of Christ. If ever man, since St. Paul, could use these words, he may, *One thing I do.*"

The voyage took Martyn down the Bay of Bengal, via Ceylon (now Sri Lanka); then northwards in the Arabian Sea, calling at Goa, where he visited the tomb of Francis Xavier, Bombay, where, on 18 February 1811, he attained the age of thirty, and Muscat in Arabia, reached just over a month later, and finally the Persian port of Bushire, where he disembarked on 22 May. After spending a week there he journeyed inland for some ten days to Shiraz and remained in that city for almost a year, expounding and discussing the Christian faith with the leaders and sages of that territory and completing his translation of the New Testament into Persian. The twelve months since his arrival in Persia had taxed him sorely. His reputation as a man of learning gained him a courteous hearing from

---

*H. C. G. Moule, *Charles Simeon* (1892; reprint London: Inter-Varsity Fellowship, 1965), p. 108.

some, but others treated him with opprobrium. On his thirty-first and last birthday (18 February 1812), when only eight chapters of the book of Revelation remained to be translated, he wrote, "Such a painful year I never passed, owing to the privations I have been called to, on the one hand, and the spectacle before me of human depravity, on the other. But I hope that I have not come to this seat of Satan in vain. The word of God has found its way into Persia, and it is not in Satan's power to oppose its progress." He had a firm confidence that the good seed thus implanted in Persian soil would not fail to yield a harvest in God's good time.

The long journey on which he now set out did nothing to improve his health. It took him by way of Isfahan and Tehran, where he was disappointed in his hope of being permitted to present a copy of his Persian New Testament to the king, and then on to Tabriz in the north, where the British ambassador, Sir Gore Ouseley, was then in residence. Altogether some thousand miles were covered in eight weeks. On 13 June, after leaving Tehran, Martyn made the following entry in his diary: "As I sat down in the dust, on the shady side of a walled village by which we passed, and surveyed the plains over which our road lay, I sighed at the thought of my dear friends in India and England, of the vast regions I must traverse before I can get to either, and of the various and unexpected hindrances which present themselves to my going forward. I comfort myself with the hope that my God has something for me to do by thus delaying my exit." As he pressed onward his strength was almost unremittingly being sapped by the rigors of the way and by extremes of heat and cold, sleeplessness, malnutrition, ague, fever, and headache; at times he was in a state of semidelirium; and often he felt himself to be more dead than alive. Arriving at Tabriz early in July, he had been reduced, as he wrote to Charles Simeon, to "a mere skeleton." There, however, the British ambassador and Lady Ouseley took him into their home and were so solicitous in their care for him that after two months he believed himself strong enough to set out on the hazardous route that had as its destination his far-distant homeland.

On 28 August 1812 he wrote in what would prove to be his last letter to Lydia Grenfell, "In three days I intend setting my horse's head towards Constantinople, distant above thirteen hundred miles"; and on 2 September he departed from Tabriz accompanied by two Armenian servants and a Turkish guide or supervisor. The latter, whom Martyn described as "the merciless Hassan," showed a callous unconcern for the young Englishman's well-being and took no account of his increasing illness and exhaustion; indeed, he hurried him on to his death through every kind of weather and at every hour of day or night. Often enough, when horses were being changed, Martyn had no better quarters in which to try to snatch a few hours rest than a corner of a stable, surrounded by the dirt and unwholesomeness of the place. A month after leaving Tabriz, forced on by Hassan, he recorded, "We flew over hill and dale to Sherean, where he changed horses. From thence we travelled all the rest of the day and all night; it rained most of the time. Soon after sunset the ague came on again, which, in my wet state, was very trying; I hardly knew how to keep my life in me." Though he was now clearly a dying man, he was compelled to move on another 170 miles along the mountain track that brought them to Tokat, in the immediate vicinity of Comana, where Chrysostom had departed this life under altogether similar circumstances. And it was there, on 16 October 1812, that this indomitable servant of God put off his "earthly tent dwelling" in the certain hope of receiving "a building from God, a house not made with hands, eternal in the heavens" (2 Cor. 5:1).

And so the histories of John Chrysostom and Henry Martyn flowed together both in the manner of their sufferings and also in the locality of their dying. In that distant neighborhood Chrysostom "turned his attention to nearby Persia and pondered on the possibility of a thorough-going Christian mission in that country."* Fourteen centuries later, Henry Martyn helped to make the patriarch's evangelistic vision a reality. On 20 September 1814, less than two years after Martyn's death, Sir Gore Ouseley sent a letter to Lord Teignmouth, the president of the British and Foreign Bible Society, to inform him that he had in person presented a copy of Martyn's Persian New Testament to the Shah, who had accepted it with graciousness and, after reading it, had written to express his admiration of the work. "In truth," the Shah

---

*H. von Campenhausen, *The Fathers of the Greek Church* (London: Adam and Charles Black, 1963), p. 156.

said, "through the learned and unremitted exertions of the Rev. Henry Martyn, it has been translated in a style most befitting sacred books, that is, in an easy and simple diction."

The number of those who have been blessed as a result of Henry Martyn's labors and afflictions is fully known elsewhere than here on earth. That there has been much fruit is not to be doubted. By way of illustration it must suffice to cite the case of a well-educated Persian gentleman who had sought out Henry Martyn when he was in Shiraz "for the purpose of treating him with scorn and exposing his doctrines to contempt." But the saintly bearing of the Englishman won his respect. "His extreme forbearance towards the violence of his opponents," this Persian subsequently declared, "the calm and yet convincing manner in which he exposed the fallacies and sophistries by which he was assailed (for he spoke Persian excellently), gradually inclined me to listen to his arguments." This man who had been trained to be a mullah became a secret believer, even avoiding Martyn's company except for visiting him to bid farewell at the time of his departure from Shiraz. "Our conversation," he wrote, "the memory of which will never fade from the tablet of my mind, sealed my conversion. He gave me a book; it has been my constant companion; the study of it has formed my most delightful occupation; its contents have often consoled me." That book was a copy of the New Testament in Persian, on a blank page of which Martyn had written, "There is joy in heaven over one sinner that repenteth."

For those who knew him it was hardly possible to speak of this godly man who had left all and given his all for Christ's cause except in superlatives. "A more perfect character I never met with, nor expect to see again on earth," Bishop Corrie said in the year after Martyn's death. And Charles Simeon in Cambridge, after reading Martyn's journal, wrote, "Truly it has humbled us all in the dust. Since the apostolic age I think that nothing has ever exceeded the wisdom and piety of our departed brother, and I conceive of no book, except the Bible, that will be found to excel this." Henry Martyn belongs to that select company of those who, ascribing everything to divine grace, have drunk the cup that the Master drank and been baptized with the baptism with which he was baptized and who now have entered into the reality of Christ's promise that "there is no one who has left house or brothers or sisters or mother or father or children or lands, for my sake and for the gospel, who will not receive a hundredfold now in this time . . . with persecutions, and in the age to come eternal life" (Mark 10:29f.).*

Today's Martyrs—"In a Severe Test of Affliction"

To imagine that Christian suffering and martyrdom belong only to the history of past ages would betray a scarcely excusable ignorance of the events and realities of our own day. Unfortunately, for those of us who live in countries where Christian discipleship is so uncostly in terms of affliction and persecution it is all too convenient to be enclosed in our freedom and to turn a deaf ear to the cries of those whose faith is being sorely tested by ungodly oppression. An abundance of evidence and documentation points to the conclusion that more Christians are suffering persecution and being cruelly put to death because of the faith they profess than at any other period in the history of the Church. The horrifying accounts of the crimes committed against humanity by the tyrants of godless Marxism have been set down in detail by Alexander Solzhenitsyn and others. The massive evidence, too little heeded, is a warning of the appalling consequences for societies and nations that are indoctrinated, not just to deny, but indeed to hate God.

In the Templeton address that he gave on 10 May 1983 in London, Solzhenitsyn declared that "the world had never before known a godlessness as organized, militarized, and tenaciously malevolent as that preached by Marxism," for, he explained, "within the philosophical system of Marx and Lenin, and at the heart of their psychology, hatred of God is the principal driving force more fundamental than all their political and economic pretensions." At the same time he solemnly warned the West that it was "ineluctably slipping toward the abyss" because of its toleration of amoral permissiveness and its derision of eternal values.

---

*For information on the life and work of Henry Martyn see *Journals and Letters of the Rev. Henry Martyn*, ed. S. Wilberforce (London: 1837); John Sargent, *The Life and Letters of Henry Martyn* (London: 1819; reprint Edinburgh: Banner of Truth Trust, 1985); George Smith, *Henry Martyn: Saint and Scholar* (London: Religious Tract Society, 1892); Richard T. France, "Henry Martyn," in *Five Pioneer Missionaries* (Edinburgh: Banner of Truth Trust, 1965; reprint 1987). The quotations in this section on Henry Martyn have been culled from the Sargent and Smith volumes.

The suffering Church is the purified Church, and its adherents are the noblest of Christians. It has no attractions for hypocrites. It is loved only by those who are filled with apostolic faith and zeal. Richard Wurmbrand, who survived fourteen years of beatings and barbarities in communist prisons, has written, "I don't feel frustrated to have lost many years in prison. I have seen beautiful things. I myself have been among the weak and insignificant ones in prison, but have had the privilege to be in the same jail with great saints, heroes of faith who equalled the Christians of the first centuries. They went gladly to die for Christ. The spiritual beauty of such saints and heroes can never be described."*

He describes how Christians arrested for worshiping in the "underground" church "wear chains with the gladness with which a bride wears a precious jewel received from her beloved."** The analogy is strongly reminiscent of the early martyrs who, according to Eusebius, "went out rejoicing, glory and grace so blended in their faces that even their bonds seemed like beautiful ornaments, like those of a bride adorned with golden finery."*** Similarly, Ignatius, martyred in Rome in A.D. 110, wrote of his bonds as "spiritual pearls";**** and Polycarp, of whom we have already given some account, spoke of those being led to martyrdom as "men encircled in saintly bonds which are the diadems of those who are truly chosen by God and our Lord."*****

Dietrich Bonhoeffer, who was imprisoned and hanged on 9 April 1945 in the tyranny of Hitler's Germany, spoke in a letter written from prison the previous August of immersing himself in the life and sufferings and death of Jesus and of his certainty that "our joy is hidden in suffering, and our life in death." On the eve of his execution, the Sunday after Easter, he conducted a service for his fellow prisoners in which he

---

*R. Wurmbrand, *Tortured for Christ* (Glendale, CA: Diane Books, 1976), p. 47.

**Ibid., p. 90.

***Eusebius, *Church History* v, 1.

****Ignatius, *Letter to the Ephesians* 11.

*****Polycarp, *Letter to the Philippians* 1.

expounded the texts of the day, namely, "with his stripes we are healed" (Isa. 53:5) and "Blessed be the God and Father of our Lord Jesus Christ! By his great mercy we have been born anew to a living hope through the resurrection of Jesus Christ from the dead" (1 Pet. 1:3). His execution took place at dawn the next day, and his last known words were, "This is the end—for me the beginning of life." Shortly beforehand the camp doctor had seen him praying in his cell, and of this he subsequently wrote, "I saw Pastor Bonhoeffer . . . kneeling on the floor praying fervently to his God. I was most deeply moved by the way this lovable man prayed, so devout and so certain that God heard his prayer."*

We should be ever thankful for the long and noble line of faithful witnesses, men, women, and children, who strengthened by divine grace have overcome temptation and endured affliction for the sake of their Redeemer. We should be fortified by their example to be steadfast in our belief and constant in the face of adversity. Like them, we too may know the power of Christ's victory in our lives, and, by virtue of the new and living way he has opened up for us into the sanctuary of God's presence, we too may draw near with boldness to the throne of grace and find grace to help in time of need. Like them, empowered by the Holy Spirit, we can joyfully proclaim the Good News to those whose minds are darkened by unbelief. And with them we will confidently look beyond the present to the imperishable inheritance that is ours in Christ, even "though now for a little while we may have to suffer various trials, so that the genuineness of our faith, more precious than gold which though perishable is tested by fire, may redound to praise and glory and honor at the revelation of Jesus Christ" (1 Pet. 1:6f.).

Let us give the last word to Thomas à Kempis (ca. 1380–1471), for the following admonition that he wrote for his day is only too appropriate for those of us who in this generation enjoy so much freedom and abundance.

---

*E. Bethge, *Dietrich Bonhoeffer* (New York: Harper and Row, 1970), pp. 829, 830.

Jesus has now many lovers of his heavenly kingdom—but few bearers of his cross. He has many that long for consolation—but few that long for tribulation. He finds many companions of his table—but few of his fast. All desire to rejoice with him—few are willing to suffer anything for him.

Many follow Jesus unto the breaking of bread—but few to the drinking of the cup of his passion. Many reverence his miracles—few follow the ignominy of his cross. Many love Jesus—so long as no adversities befall. Many praise and bless him—so long as they receive consolations from him. But if Jesus hide himself but a little while—they fall either into complaining or into great dejection.

But they who love Jesus for the sake of Jesus, and not for some special comfort of their own, bless him in all tribulation and distress of heart as well as in the dearest comfort. Yea though he should never choose to give them comfort, yet would they ever praise him and wish to be always giving thanks.*

---

*Thomas à Kempis, *The Imitation of Christ* ii, 11. I have followed Charles Bigg's translation (London: Methuen, 1908), pp. 124f.